Points + Lines

Points+

Stan Allen

Princeton Architectural Press New York

Lines

DIAGRAMS AND PROJECTS FOR THE CITY

PUBLISHED BY

Princeton Architectural Press

37 East Seventh Street

New York, NY 10003

For a catalog of books published
by Princeton Architectural Press,
call toll free 1.800.722.6657 or visit www.papress.com

EDITOR: Mark Lamster

JACKET DESIGN: Stan Allen and Sara E. Stemen

BOOK DESIGN: Stan Allen and Sara E. Stemen

SPECIAL THANKS: Eugenia Bell, Jane Garvie, Caroline Green,
Clare Jacobson, Therese Kelly, and Annie Nitschke of Princeton
Architectural Press   —Kevin C. Lippert, publisher

PRINTED AND BOUND IN CHINA

LIBRARY OF CONGRESS CATALOGING−IN−PUBLICATION DATA

Allen, Stan.

   Points + lines : diagrams and projects for the city / Stan
Allen.

    p. cm.

   Includes biographical references.

   ISBN 1-56898-155-4 (pbk. : alk. paper)

   1. Allen, Stan — Themes, motives. 2. Architecture, Modern—20th century—Themes, motives. 3. Architectural practice, International.   I. Title. II. Title: Points and lines.

NA737.A44A4 1999

720/ .92—dc21   98-38817

                                   CIP

BACKROUND: fiction/nonfiction Gallery, New York, 1991

Stations and paths together form a system. Points and lines, beings and relations. What is interesting might be the construction of the system, the number and disposition of stations and paths. Or it might be the flow of messages passing through the lines. In other words, a complex system can be formally described.... One might have sought the formation and distribution of the lines, paths, and stations, their borders, edges and forms. But one must write as well of the interceptions, of the accidents in the flow along the way between stations.... What passes may be a message but static prevents it from being heard, and sometimes, from being sent.   —Michel Serres

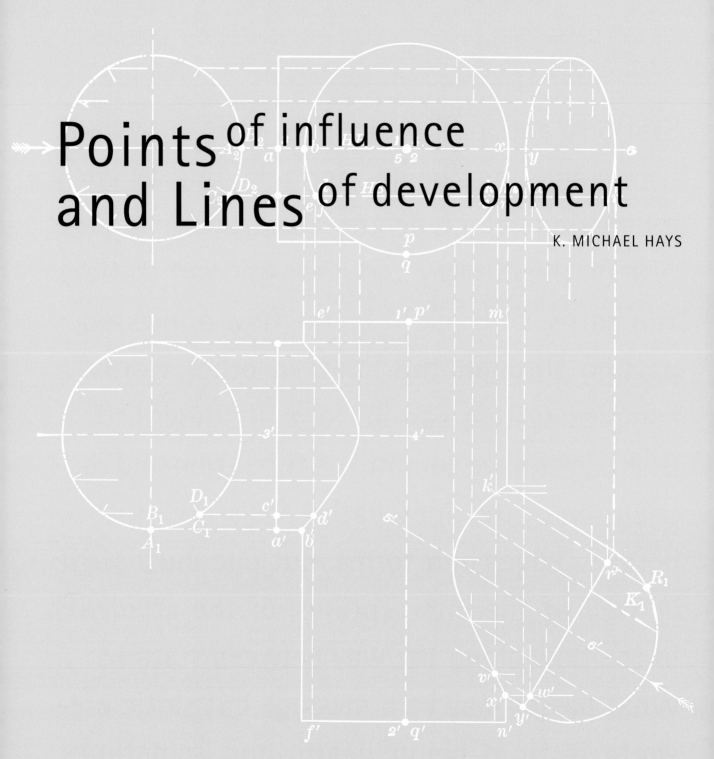

Points of influence
and Lines of development

K. MICHAEL HAYS

Before they actually met, Jeffrey Kipnis once remarked that, judging from his CV, Stan Allen must be either much older than he looks or very confused. Allen's experiences include not only a large number of connections to people and institutions in the architectural world, connections that usually take some time to make, but also some that don't seem to quite line up on any continuous ideological curve. Schooled at Brown, the Institute for Architecture and Urbanism, Cooper Union (where he was under the tutelage of Bernard Tschumi as well as John Hejduk), and Princeton (in 1987–88, a crucial moment of transition for that school), he has worked for Diana Agrest and Mario Gandelsonas, Rafael Moneo, and Richard Meier, taught at Harvard and Columbia, written forty or so articles of criticism and theory, exhibited his own work in both architecture schools and art galleries, has himself built projects for both architecture schools and art galleries, and, well, maybe Jeff was right? While no one *should* be reduced to their formative influences, everyone, of course, *can* be. Or almost. The various, often conflicting discourses from which Stan Allen's work has emerged provide a key, by way of introduction to the projects and texts presented here, to at least a partial understanding of his overall project.

In the mid- to late 1970s the Institute for Architecture and Urban Studies was an extraordinary apparatus for the distillation of architectural theory, a decantation chamber where the semiotic studies of Diana Agrest and Mario Gandelsonas, the culture industry analysis of Kenneth Frampton, the Foucauldian nineteenth-century historical and typological work of Anthony Vidler, and the formal research of Peter Eisenman all blended and swirled around a critique of modernism and new concerns about meaning in architecture. Through the institute also flowed Rosalind Krauss's reformulation of the terms of minimalism, the negative thought of Manfredo Tafuri, and the first American glimpses of the work of Aldo Rossi. In different ways and to different degrees, all of these discourses figure into Allen's work, or better, the working though of these discourses does, for none of these lines of thought are left untransformed. Rather their coordination requires that questions of formal meaning be deposed by questions about the effect or performance of formal organizations, both semiotic and material; that strategies of negation give way to strategies for enabling alternative uses and conceptualizations; and that typological analyses yield to cartography. The constellation that comprises the second of each of these terms is already a rough sketch of what Allen calls "field conditions."

At Cooper Union in the 1980s architecture seemed to draw strength from its original sin of the division of manual and mental labor. To deny the separation and fake an integration (for any such integration could be only fake) was a regression, not a solution. And yet, perspective, the traditional penance for that sin and the primary device for tying an architect's visions to the real, found its filaments unraveling, its precision blunted like any overused instrument. At Cooper Union, the process of

1

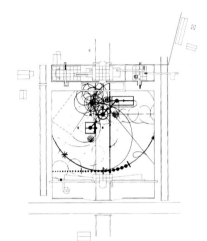

"Theater of Production,"
Cooper Union thesis, 1981.

It risks little to assert that among the most pondered issues in architecture today is the production of effects—the arrangement and distribution of experiential content and expressive content through architectural form. The range of this issue extends from carefully fabricated building details intended to coax out the latent, contradictory, and marginal aesthetic effects of constructed materials to complex, large-scale geometrical systems that promote differentiated forms and structures for programmatic activities. In distinction to "stronger" but narrower models such as functionalism or formalism, the notion of architecture as the production of effects is often associated with "minor" or "marginal" practices, with the consequence that, in some circles, the analysis of effects has all but displaced the concern with form in the conventional sense.

Allen's more recent efforts surely coincide with this interest in architecture as effect, but his attitude toward form is more particular. "Form matters, but more for what it can do than for what it looks like," he declares. Or alternatively, "Form matters, but not so much the form of things as the forms *between* things." This attitude seems to me a logical progression from a general concern with the scene of production to this more particular, strategic space between the built thing and the uses it then enables and supports: forms between things constitute a site for actions, a staging of a vantage ground from which effects are launched. Neither function nor

retooling architecture's templates of the real involved the renunciation of perspective in favor of various other notational and cartographic systems. Bernard Tschumi's first-hand knowledge of performance art and his interest in the event-space of architecture—a way of practicing space related to both Georges Bataille's *expérience intérieure* and the Situationists' *événements*—found support in Hejduk's Cooper Union and Hejduk's own interest in traditions of folklore, carnivals, and masques. And architectural drawing came to be understood as a kind of choreography—a graphic system that could map the very psychogeography of the city. All of these elements were synthesized in Allen's bachelor's thesis at Cooper Union (of 1981, the same year, interestingly enough, as the publication of Tschumi's *Manhattan Transcripts*). The title of the thesis was "The Theater of Production," underscoring the interest both in the process and the scene of action and effects.

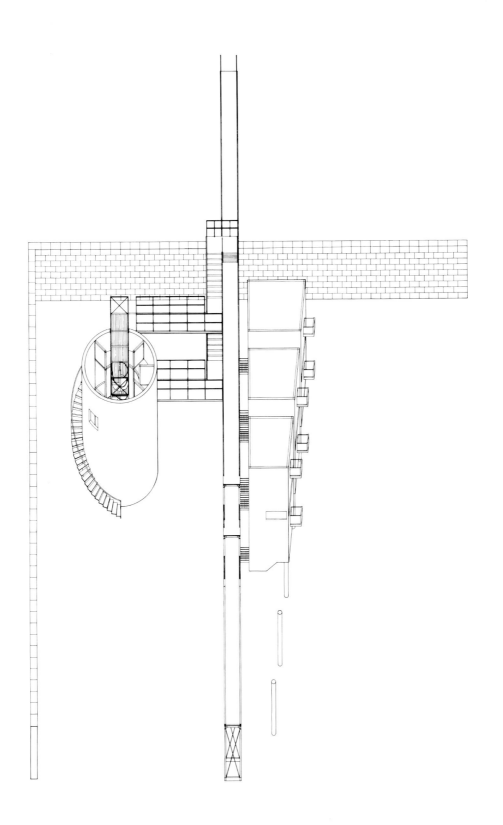

"Theater of Production." Axonometric of artists' housing

form is abandoned. Rather, form is reconceptualized as a condition conducive to certain outcomes, certain possibilities of activity and habitation. Form is an instigator of performances and responses, a frame that suggests rather than fixes, that maps or diagrams possibilities that will be realized only partially at any one time.

If the provenance of semiotics and negative thought is properly located in the 1970s rewriting of modernist aesthetics, something like the binary logic of semiotics and the negativity of modernist aesthetics still bleeds through the fabric of recent theories that claim a more radically proliferated and destabilizing force. In most versions of architecture under the Derridean influence (I'm resisting calling it deconstructivist), the negativity of the modern avant-garde remains but is reconstituted as a specific sign system in its own right, which is then "critically," even "violently," opposed (remember how much those words were used in the eighties?) to the context into which it is inserted. The strident freshness of the new architecture still seeks to perform an essentially modernist function of renewal of perception. But it substitutes for modernism's totalized socioaesthetic, productive package, a practice of signs that shares the same techniques of building production and delivery with *another* practice of signs that it opposes.

As early as 1986, Allen had already assimilated (from Paul Virilio, Michel Foucault, and others) the fact that, in the face of electronic communication, air travel, global financial markets,

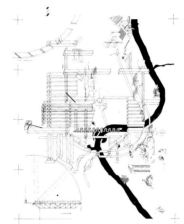

LEFT: "Piranesi Campo Marzio: An Experimental Design," 1986–89. Site axonometric

OPPOSITE: "Scoring the City," The London Project (with Marc Hacker), 1986.

5

and the like, it would be a combination of naiveté and hubris to think that traditional architectural semiotics could any longer manage mass communication and perception. Not as a proposed solution but as an expanded cartography for understanding this condition, *Scoring the City*, executed in collaboration with Marc Hacker, juxtaposed simultaneous and incommensurable presentations of cultural, temporal, and spatial information—including time zones, aircraft navigational charts, images from advertising and stock markets, and underground transportation diagrams—in order to register the complexity of cognizing the global representational territory architecture would henceforth have to reckon with. In 1989, Allen's more tactical textualization of Piranesi's *Campo Marzio*, what he called an "excavation—through drawing and writing—

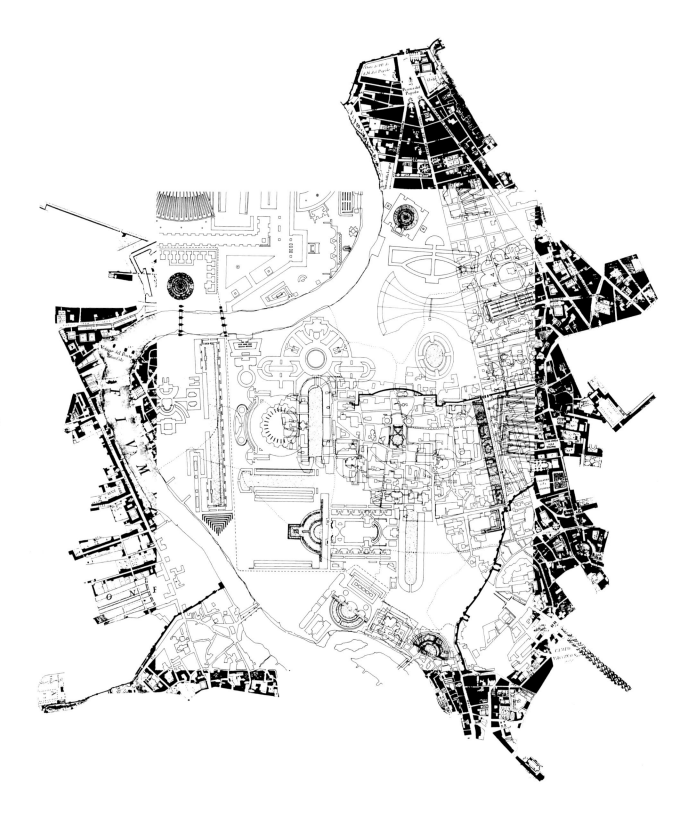

6

Points of Influence and Lines of Development   K. MICHAEL HAYS

of the 'negative utopia' drawn by Piranesi," recoded Piranesi's own ideological mapping of Rome through Man Ray's *Dust Breeding* (itself a recoding of Duchamp's *Large Glass* insofar as it turns the Large Glass into a temporal landscape), in what can already be seen as a postcollage field condition, a highly charged *dispositif* that first deterritorializes, then reaccumulates the asignifying and nonrepresentative borders, frames, and figures that serialize and superimpose possibilities of program, possibilities of fact.

Allen's first built works seem, on a gloss, to depart from issues of notation and framing, and mark what will become an ongoing interest in minimalism. Surely the architecture of the small galleries in Manhattan done around 1990 is minimal in the grossest sense of the term. But a statement of Allen's made around the time these projects were designed already inter-

cepts and redirects our first tendency to look in these galleries for a simple minimalist aesthetic: "The minimal language of the projects…should not be misunderstood. The claim is not for unmediated presence or for the 'specificity' of the object [à la Donald Judd]. I am interested in a minimal language not for its materiality but for its immateriality; not in the clarification of form but in its dissolution; not in what is revealed but in what is covered up; not in self-sufficiency but in incompleteness." What joins and reconciles these projects with Allen's earlier research into the notation of architecture's infrastructural dimension is not minimalism's objective materiality but what Michael Fried disparagingly called minimalism's literalism and incurable theatricality (think again of the "theater of production"), which is "concerned with the actual circumstances in which the beholder encounters literalist work.…The experience of literalist art is of an object in a *situation*."[1] Referring to a story told by Tony Smith about a nighttime ride with some students on the still unfinished New Jersey Turnpike in the early 1950s (a story Allen has often referred to), Fried underscores how minimalism seduces through its banality and the lowness of its address. Smith:

> It was a dark night and there were no lights or shoulder markers, lines, railings, or anything at all except the dark pavement moving through the landscape of the flats, rimmed by hills in the distance, but punctuated by stacks, towers, fumes, and

7

Able House (project),
1991–92. Construc-
tion model

8

colored lights....It seemed that there had been a reality there that had not had any expression in art.

The experience of the road was something mapped out but not socially recognized. I thought to myself, it ought to be clear that's the end of art. Most painting looks pretty pictorial after that. There is no way you can frame it, you just have to experience it.[2]

Allen switches the valence of Fried's analysis of minimalism from negative to positive. What Allen draws from minimalism is its disruption of formal autonomy ("you just have to experience it"); its relation of situation, performance, and notation ("the experience of the road was something mapped out," punctuated by infrastructural props, lighting, movement, and bodies); and a programmatic latency that remains unannounced, perhaps even unformed, but is nevertheless spatialized, future-directed, and inescapably social ("mapped out but not socially recognized"). And while Smith finds "there is no way you can frame it," that is, hang minimalist experience on a wall and thereby sanction it institutionally, Allen insists that its very lack of determinacy, its doubt, produces its own frame, or better, a field condition. Conventional architectural compositions and even "decompositions" (as Eisenman once experimented with) can at most estrange architecture from itself by subverting its founding assumptions in an endless process of dismantlement and reinstitutionalization; they cannot be both *of* architecture and *in advance of* architecture's uses in the present as a felt moment of historical time. Yet field conditions can be, through their metonymic emission of multiple simultaneous performance vectors and programmatic surfaces, often conflicting and always in different rhythms and relations.

The American city is itself only the most obvious manifestation of a field condition: an enormous deterritorialized plane, its boundaries contingent on a particular geography and topography (stopped by a river or mountain range or an arbitrarily legislated property line), reterritorialized by any of various patterns (grids, patchworks, mosaics), some of which are inscribed on the ground, many of which may lie beneath the thin, occupiable surface, insensible yet controlling—infrastructural points and lines of force whose positions and relations have been determined by a notational language conventionally understood and translated by the multiple agents responsible for putting them in place. As much as by the partitioning off of areas, the type and intensity of activity on the surface is regulated by a kind of rheostatic apparatus below that also senses changes on the surface it now charges (we need more cable here, another tunnel there). The bodies on the surface are so many metal filings on a plate, forming patterns (flocks, swarms, neighborhoods), which are also charged with group alliances and specific cognitive and practical ways of negotiating the templates that enable possible performative events.

Understood in this way, Allen's field condition is also available for conceptualizing conditions different from the modern city's culture of congestion—edge cities, suburbs, "West Coast urbanism," the "thick two-dimensions" of Asian cities, and others; it is a docket of the emergent posturban life that has heretofore seemed unmappable and unmanageable. A practical, architectural construction of such conditions is what Stan Allen's work promises. Most architecture looks pretty pictorial after that.

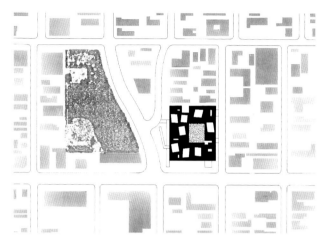

Korean-American Museum of Art, 1995. Site plan

9

NOTES

1. Michael Fried, *Art and Objecthood* (Chicago: The University of Chicago Press, 1998), 153.
2. Tony Smith, cited in ibid., 157–8.

Contextual

"Montage is the determination of the whole...

by means of continuities, cutting and false continuities."

PROJECTS

Cardiff Bay Opera House, Cardiff, Wales, 1994

Museo del Prado, Madrid, 1995/98

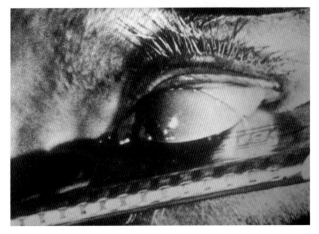

TOP: Dziga Vertov, *Man with a Movie Camera*, 1928. Still

BOTTOM: Luis Buñuel and Salvador Dalí, *Un Chien Andalou*, 1929. Still

"But what characterizes the montage and hence its role as a cell or movie frame? The collision—the conflict of two opposing pieces." SERGEI EISENSTEIN, 1929

01 MONTAGE PRACTICES: THE METROPOLIS

Early modernist methodologies of collage and montage acquired force through the collision of distinct orders and the generation of tension across seams of difference. Difference was encoded in forceful juxtaposition. Anticipating the modernist fascination with collision, symbolist poet Isidore Ducasse (the "comte de Lautréamont") spoke of the terrifying beauty produced by the intersection of "...the sewing machine and the umbrella on the dissecting table." In the case of Soviet filmmaker Dziga Vertov montage has another, more politically charged function. Sudden and unexpected juxtapositions dislocate the spectator's habits of perception. The artificial spell of the cinema is momentarily broken in order to "lay bare" the device of its own construction. Filmmaking is shown to be work like any other: the repetitive spinning motions of splicing or editing are intercut with images of wool spinning, printing presses, and other manufacturing processes. Stop motion freezes the flow of time, reminding the viewer that his own subjectivity collaborates in the construction of the movie's artifice.

Vertov's political and technological optimism contrasts with the sense of absurdity expressed in *Un Chien Andalou*, the 1929 film made by Luis Buñuel and Salvador Dali. Here the violence of modern metropolitan life comes to the surface, expressing both the escalation necessary to maintain the shock effect, and the loss of faith in a progressive and redemptive modernism. Surrealism erodes modernism from within, registering an emergent awareness that the whole hygienic-panoptic project of modernism—its desire to remake the world on the basis of new technologies—contains within it the potential to go disastrously wrong.

Architecture is of course more intimately linked to normative constraints of economic and technical reality than these experimental films, and at the same time less sensitive to the speculations of the avant-garde. Yet in the proposals of Mies van der Rohe for urban buildings in the 1920s, analagous aesthetic of disjunctive effects is evident. His 1928 project for the remodeling of the Alexanderplatz in Berlin, sets a series of crystalline geometric solids against the complex and heterogeneous mix of the late nineteenth-century city fabric. The buildings are marked by the nature of the new metropolis. As objects, they embody the logic of new technologies and changed subjectivities. Yet they also stand apart from the chaos of the city to offer a critique, to point elsewhere. It is no accident that this project is represented by means of photo montage. Through the very means of representation itself, Mies makes explicit the seams, gaps, and distractions of modern metropolitan life.[1] It is worth noting, however, that in Mies's collage disjunction exists not internal to the architecture itself, but *between* the architecture and its context. Mies has established complex and discontinuous relationships between a series of objects that are

Mies van der Rohe, Alexanderplatz, Berlin, 1928. Photomontage

themselves fundamentally regular—even geometrically pure—and a city fabric characterized by impure mixtures of old and new. As a result of the uneven implementation of modern technologies in the early twentieth-century metropolis, the traditional and the modern tended already to coexist in disjunctive proximity. It is this condition that Mies has made visible in his project.

02 AFTER THE METROPOLIS

Among the diverse and multiple definitions of postmodernity, the loss of difference consistently emerges as a theme: modernity's capacity to shock has given way to effects of leveling, the dominance of abstract values, a loss of depth, what Jean-François

TOP: Office Building,
Metropark, New Jersey

BOTTOM: Tokyo street at
night

regard to housing and community all tended to move the city away from density, and to dilute its complex mixtures. As Marc Hacker has pointed out, this dismantling of urban density was motivated in large part by Cold War fears of nuclear attack.[4] The metropolis—once a dense punctual locus of urban identity, privileged site of the encounter with the other—has faded from view, replaced by a vast megalopolis interconnected by communication networks both physical and virtual.

Jameson's loss of "depth" or Lyotard's "slackening" therefore have very real counterparts in contemporary urban experience. The city today is experienced as a field of ineffable effects suspended in an ether of immaterial signs. These signs differ from one another not in substance, but in meaning. The "waning of affect" is in part visible in the collapse of regional identity and a corresponding loss of a sense of place. Meaningful social and political differences have been evened out. In the politics of culture, this leads to a loss of the avant-garde's special capacity—as privileged avatar of "otherness"—to measure and mark those differences. The margins have been incorporated into the mainstream, and the possibility of standing outside has been eroded by the leveling effect of new technologies. As we move from an economy dominated by technologies of production to an economy dominated by technologies of reproduction, the differences between *things* seem less significant that the potential sameness of *images*. In the postmodern world of simulation, anything can combine with anything else without producing a sense of shock.

Lyotard described as a "slackening" and what Fredric Jameson called the "waning of affect."[2] This is no doubt in part an effect of new digital technologies that reconfigure concrete objects as abstract information. Distraction, which once implied a radical model for new subjectivities, becomes empty time. Sergei Eisenstein's explosive discontinuities fade to Gilles Deleuze's "false continuities."

What has changed in the new urbanism of the periphery—sometimes designated as "edge city"[3]—is not so much the nature of the object as its context. During the postwar period in the United States, massive decentralization, the construction of an interstate highway infrastructure, and new expectations with

Shinto priests blessing fighter jet

Digital technologies facilitate the seamless combination of images from different sources. Further, the nature of digital media itself functions to even out the differences previously emphasized by collage and montage practices. As Vivian Sobchack has pointed out: "Digital electronic technology atomizes and *abstractly schematizes* the analogic quality of the photographic and cinematic into discrete *pixels* and *bits* of information that are transmitted *serially*, each bit discontinuous, discontiguous, and absolute—each bit 'being in itself' even as it is part of a system."[5] A field of immaterial ciphers is substituted for the material traces of the object. Media theorist Friedrich Kittler has pointed out that with the emergence of digital technologies—where sound, images, or text are all converted into digital code—the differences between media themselves (and the corresponding concept of "multimedia") disappear: "The general digitalization of information and channels erases the difference between individual media. Sound and image, voice and text have become mere effects on the surface, or, to put it better, the interface for the consumer."[6] Hierarchies are distributed; "value" is evened out. Digital ciphers differ one from the other only as place holders in a code.

A number of ostensibly opposed positions have emerged among architects who have addressed the pervasive role of media and technology in the city today. One asserts that architecture will fade away under the advancing imperatives of technology. Under the domain of distraction, media and technology threaten architecture with its own obsolescence. This has led some architects to retrench, and insist ever more stridently on architecture's material specificity. Others submit to the imperatives of the new technologies and redefine architecture as media and image. Alternatively, architects have attempted to reassert architecture's traditional capacity to represent (formally or metaphorically) the condition of distraction through a fragmented or "dislocated" architecture that stands as the metaphoric equivalent to the dizzy euphoria of communication. In each case, architecture is understood as something different from media, its physicality opposed to the virtual effects of media and digital technology.

Architectural work by its nature endorses the value of the physical over the virtual. Yet if understood simply as a form of resistance to the virtual, architecture risks its own marginalization.

15

The capacity to actualize the virtual is a fundamental and even traditional aspect of architecture. From the manipulation of light and space in the work of Francesco Borromini or Guarino Guarini, to the fugitive tectonic effects of Mies van der Rohe, to the extensive spatial elaborations of Hans Scharoun, architecture's tangible presence is always informed by a corresponding virtual field. Shifting relations of program, information, and use further extend architecture's engagement with the invisible flows of the city. Architecture is already marked by complex relations of real to virtual. Only by creatively examining the role of the architect in these changing urban economies can architecture evolve the means to reengage the world.

03 CONTEXTUAL TACTICS: FIVE PROPOSITIONS

The projects illustrated here register a shift from a late-modernist project of fragmentation (characterized by the aesthetics of disjunction and its associated critical discourses) toward an architecture of continuity and connectivity, lightness and affect. Beginning with the detailed specifics of program or site, these projects work incrementally toward the definition of a new urban condition. In each case, a loosely defined envelope or field supports a high degree of diversity, exchange and complexity. This is more than a stylistic shift: it is an architecture that functions smoothly without necessarily looking smooth.

1. INTENSIVE PROGRAMMING

Prevailing linguistic models of reception, and a concomitant emphasis on visuality, have enforced the idea of architecture as a discursive practice. But spatial practices both precede and exceed discursive practices. Architectural subjects are users as well as spectators, participants as well as readers. In practice, this implies intensive programming, but also an elastic yet precise relation between spatial accommodation and formal invention; a loose fit between event and structure.

2. DISTRACTION (SLACKENING)

Given the evident ineffectiveness of strategies of unmasking, disavowal, or defamiliarization in a state of distraction, I would propose instead the appropriation and redirection of the very technologies of distraction enforced by dominant culture. We can't simply criticize distraction in the hope of recovering some notion of authentic experience. We need strategies of intensification, not strategies of delay. The radical gesture today is not to unmask, or to resist the simulacrum, but rather to require the simulacrum, against all expectation, to function as the real. Camouflage, mimicry, wit, guileful ruse, deception, and stealth—"tricky and stubborn procedures that elude discipline without being outside the field in which it is exercised"—enter the catalog of architectural means to reprogram the dominant logics of space in the city.[7]

3. SITE ACCOMMODATION

In the urban realm this implies the resolution of site conditions through accommodation, not conflict, juxtaposition, and fragmentation (buildings that are evolved, not designed). Contextual tactics treat constraints as opportunity, and move away from a modernist ethic—and aesthetics—of transgression. Working with and not against the site, something new is produced by registering the complexity of the given.

4. FIELD CONDITIONS

Form matters, but not so much the forms of things as the forms *between* things.

5. POSTCOLLAGE

Collage and montage acquired force through the collision of distinct orders and the generation of tension across seams of difference. Previously stable subjectivities were fragmented. But today mobile subjectivities can be put into play both with and against existing spatial orders. The disjunctive play of difference has lost the power to shock. Fluid models of exchange, differential unities and free floating intensities replace the critical model of recuperating difference through ever escalating fragmentation.

NOTES

1. See K. Michael Hays, *Modernism and the Post-Humanist Subject* (Cambridge, MA: MIT Press, 1993) or the essays collected in Detlef Mertins, ed., *The Presence of Mies* (New York: Princeton Architectural Press, 1994).

2. See Jean-François Lyotard, "Answering the Question: 'What is Postmodernism?'" in *The Postmodern Condition* (Minneapolis, MN: University of Minnesota Press, 1986); Fredric Jameson, "Postmodernism, or the Cultural Logic of Late Capitalism," *New Left Review* 146 (1984): 53–92.

3. See, among others, Joel Garreau, *Edge City: Life on the New Frontier* (New York: Doubleday, 1991).

4. Marc Hacker "Notes on a Changed World," *Perspecta* 21 (1983).

5. Vivian Sobchak, "The Scene of the Screen: Towards a Phenomenology of Cinematic and Electronic Presence," in *Post-Script* 10 (1990): 56.

6. Friedrich A. Kittler "Gramophone, Film, Typewriter" in *Literature, Media, Information Systems*, ed. John Johnstone (Newark, NJ: G+B Arts International, 1997), 31–2.

7. Michel de Certeau, *The Practice of Everyday Life* (Berkeley: University of California Press, 1986), 96.

Cardiff Bay Opera House, Cardiff, Wales

COMPETITION, 1994

ARCHITECT: Stan Allen

ASSISTED BY Jack Phillips, Katherine Kim

To make a space for public spectacle today demands the rethinking of the traditional representation of the opera house. We proposed a building that would give generous public spaces back to the city in order to make the opera an integral part of modern urban life while at the same time incorporating the building into the site's history as former shipyards and docks. In the massing and organization of the building, we elected to give equal importance to the support spaces—both technical (workshops, rehearsal spaces, etc.) and administrative. In this way the building celebrates the production of the spectacle as much as its consumption.

BUILDING ORGANIZATION

A clearly formed auditorium block articulates the hierarchies of the program and creates a focal point for the Cardiff waterfront. An "L" shaped boardwalk, one level up, overlooks the city's Oval Basin and links the opera house to a proposed boulevard and the surrounding urban fabric through a sequence of public circulation spaces. The ground level concourse is entered directly from Pierhead Street and

RIGHT: **Program distribution**

OPPOSITE: **Sketch: program/service**

View of Cardiff

from the Oval Basin. Workshops, offices, and rehearsal spaces located on upper floors wrap the auditorium to form an open network of workspaces throughout the site.

In addition to the boardwalk, which gives access to public restaurants and the auditorium foyer, a ground floor concourse adjacent to the Oval Basin and Pierhead Street connects directly to the parking areas. Glazed with a serpentine wall, this space will provide a lively public amenity capable of functioning independent of the opera house itself. The upper levels, poised between the glass skin of the building and the sculptural body of the auditorium, command impressive views over the bay.

The scale of the building suggests a vessel in dry-dock. Its massing derives not from honorific or symbolic considerations, but rather articulates the complexity of the given program. The functional interrelation of orchestra, stage, fly tower, and rehearsal stages are clearly registered in the external massing. The distinct scales of production spaces and administrative offices are legible in the sectional treatment of the support wing. Public spaces, in turn, link back to local city functions and assure that the site will be active twenty-four hours a day.

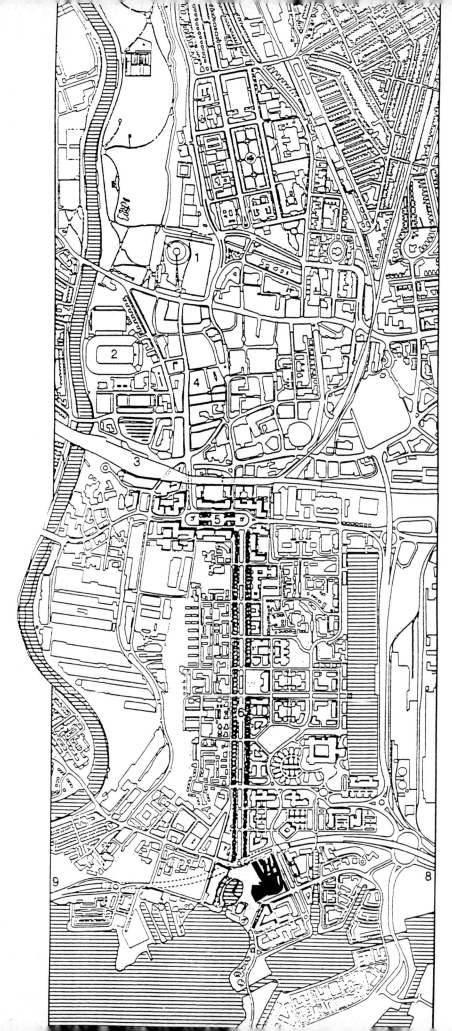

RIGHT: Urban context

OPPOSITE: Site axonometric

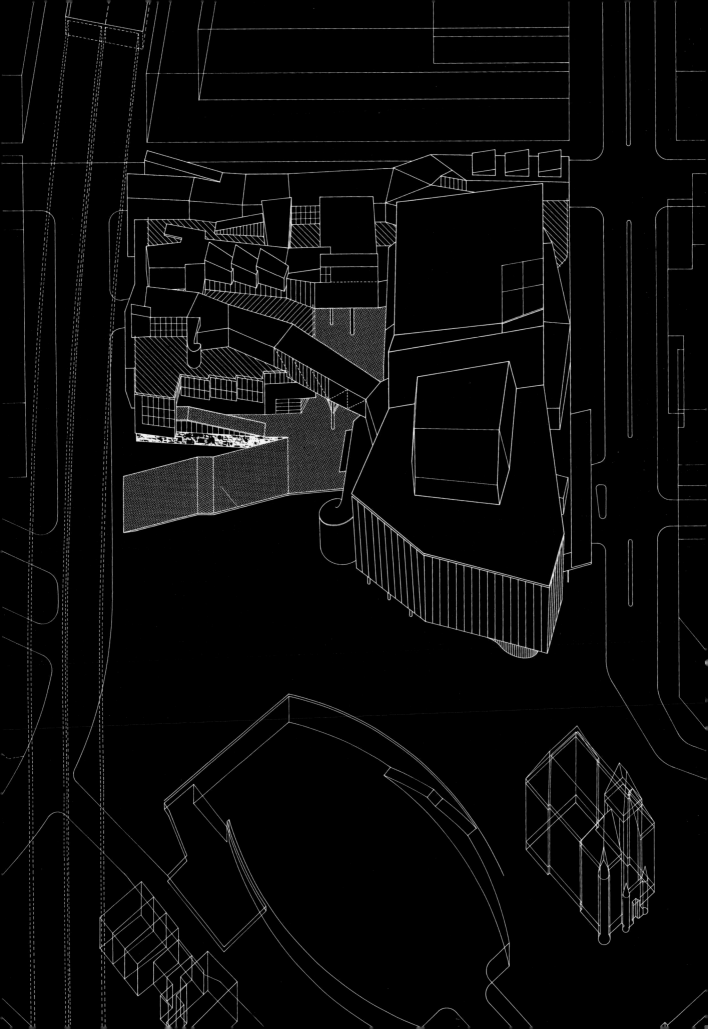

ABOVE: Massing model

OPPOSITE: Site plan

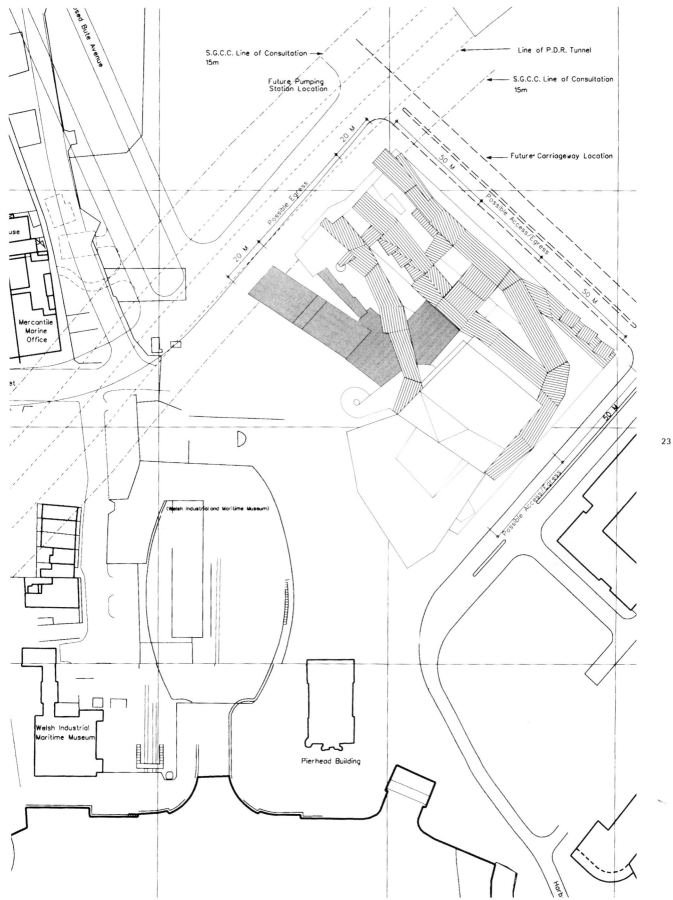

S.G.C.C. Line of Consultation
15m

Line of P.D.R. Tunnel

Future Pumping
Station Location

S.G.C.C. Line of Consultation
15m

Future Carriageway Location

Possible Egress

20 M

20 M

50 M

Possible Access/Egress

50 M

Possible Access/Egress

50 M

23

Mercantile
Marine
Office

(Welsh Industrial and Maritime Museum)

Welsh Industrial
Maritime Museum

Pierhead Building

Harb

sed Bute Avenue

Model view (city side)

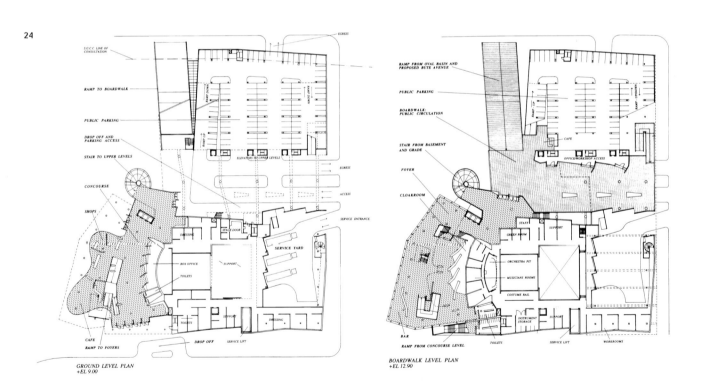

Plan: ground level

Plan: boardwalk level

Model view (plaza side)

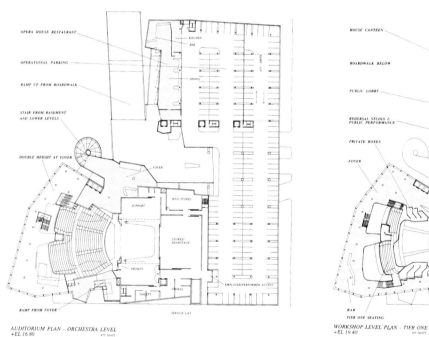

AUDITORIUM PLAN - ORCHESTRA LEVEL
+EL 16.80

Plan: orchestra level

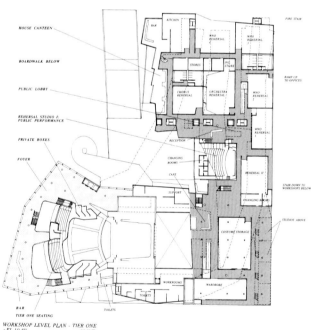

WORKSHOP LEVEL PLAN - TIER ONE
+EL 19.40

Plan: workshop level

ABOVE: **Model view (water side)**

OPPOSITE: **Model view in context**

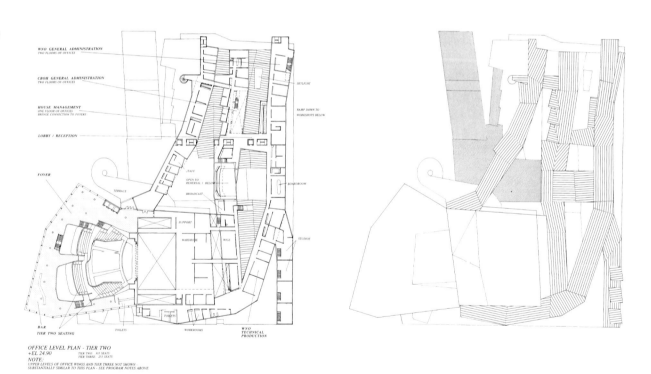

WNO GENERAL ADMINISTRATION
TWO FLOORS OF OFFICES

CBOH GENERAL ADMINISTRATION
TWO FLOORS OF OFFICES

HOUSE MANAGEMENT
ONE FLOOR OF OFFICES
BRIDGE CONNECTION TO FOYERS

LOBBY / RECEPTION

FOYER

TERRACE

STAFF

OPEN TO
REHEARSAL 1 BELOW

BROADCAST

SUPPORT

WARDROBE   WIGS

BAR
TIER TWO SEATING

TOILETS   WORKROOMS

SKYLIGHT

RAMP DOWN TO
WORKSHOPS BELOW

BOARDROOM

STUDIOS

WNO
TECHNICAL
PRODUCTION

OFFICE LEVEL PLAN - TIER TWO
+EL 24.90   TIER TWO   105 SEATS
                     TIER THREE 255 SEATS
NOTE:
UPPER LEVELS OF OFFICE WINGS AND TIER THREE NOT SHOWN
SUBSTANTIALLY SIMILAR TO THIS PLAN - SEE PROGRAM NOTES ABOVE

Plan: office level

Plan: roof

28

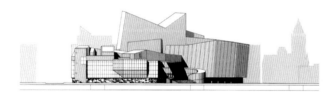

TOP: Cross-section (auditorium)

BOTTOM: City elevation

TOP: Water elevation

BOTTOM: Cross-section (entry/boardwalk)

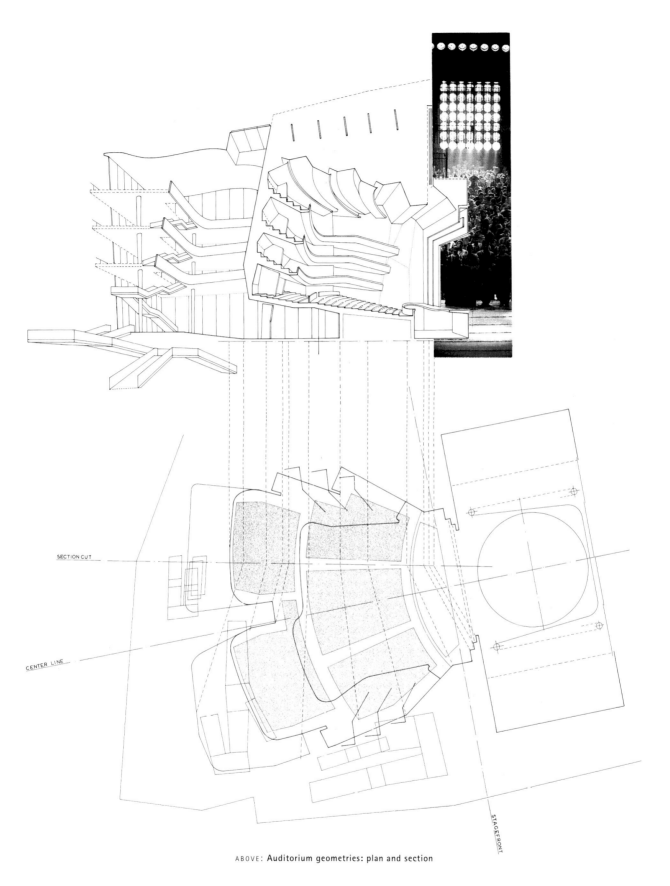

SECTION CUT

CENTER LINE

STAGE FRONT

ABOVE: Auditorium geometries: plan and section

Contextual Tactics CARDIFF

Extension of the Museo del Prado, Madrid

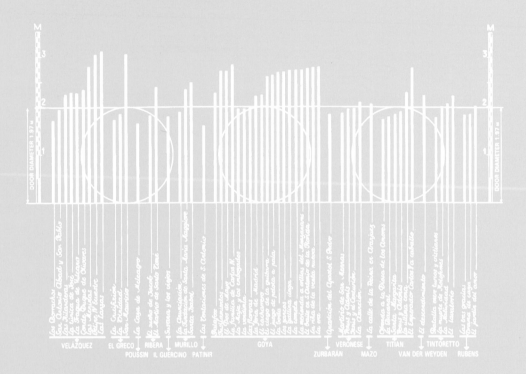

COMPETITION: **1995**; REWORKED: **1998**

ARCHITECT: Stan Allen

ASSISTED BY: Andrew Burgess, and Martin Felsen (1995) /

Chris Perry, Marcel Baumgartner (1997–98)

In 1995, the Museo del Prado in Madrid held a competition for proposals to unify its separate buildings: the original, eighteenth-century Juan de Villanueva Building; the Cason del Buen Retiro, where Pablo Picasso's *Guernica* is displayed; and the Military Museum. As such, the brief presented an opportunity to rethink the place of the institution in the urban fabric. Traditionally, the museum has been seen as a place set apart from the liveliness of the city. Recognizing the city as the extended field of the new museum, however, we proposed to organize the new construction around the expression of the museum's public spaces rather than attempt to recenter the museum complex around a central building or "figure." The extension was conceived as a continuation of the botanical gardens bordering the site to the south. Its organization mediates between the hard geometries of the adjacent urban blocks and the softer patterns of the gardens. The extension redefines the new museum as an open institution, a blank slate on which all the complexity of life in the modern city may be newly imprinted.

In order to establish a place for public functions on a site without clear architectural limits, a decisive intervention was required. In a gesture of respect to the original fabric of the Villanueva Building, we began our work by stripping away its various twentieth-century accretions. In this way, a new site for the museum was created behind the existing building while preserving the historic view of the front façade from the Paseo del Prado, Madrid's tree-lined central boulevard.

A gentle ramp connects the Paso del Prado to the new entry, giving access to a continuous public concourse that connects the new museum functions. Each of these (entry and auditorium, temporary galleries and research library) receives individual expression in the form of a translucent, double-skinned pavilion, while the flowing roof of the concourse, a densely planted garden surface, serves to unify these cubic structures. Service and support functions are arrayed in the spaces between pavilions. Instead of being built over, as proposed in the competition brief, the Cloister of San Jeronimo is restored and returned to the city as a public garden overlooking the museum complex.

31

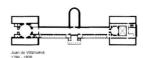

Juan de Villanueva
1786 - 1808

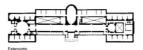

Extensions
1914 - 1918

Existing building and
previous extensions

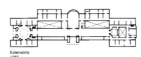

Extensions
1955

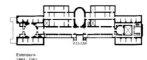

Extensions
1964 - 1967

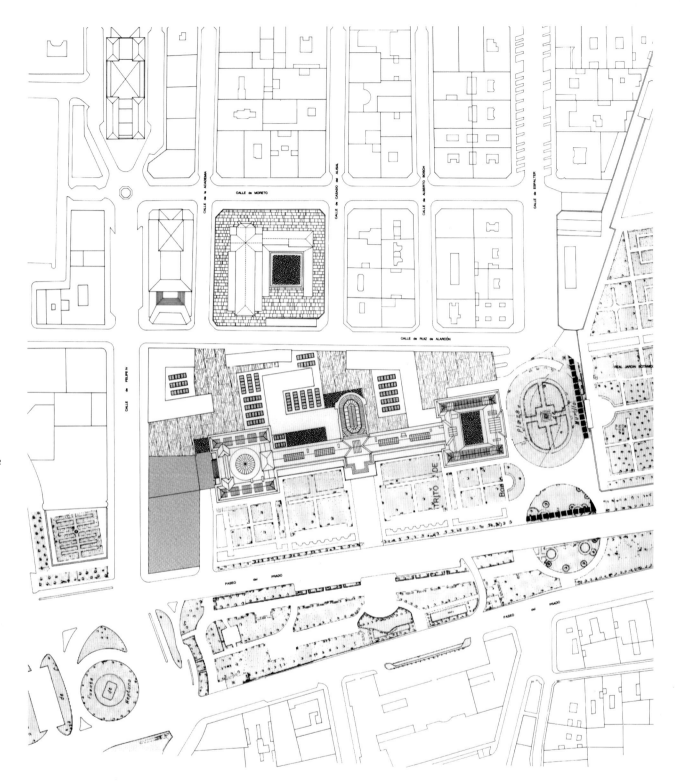

Context plan

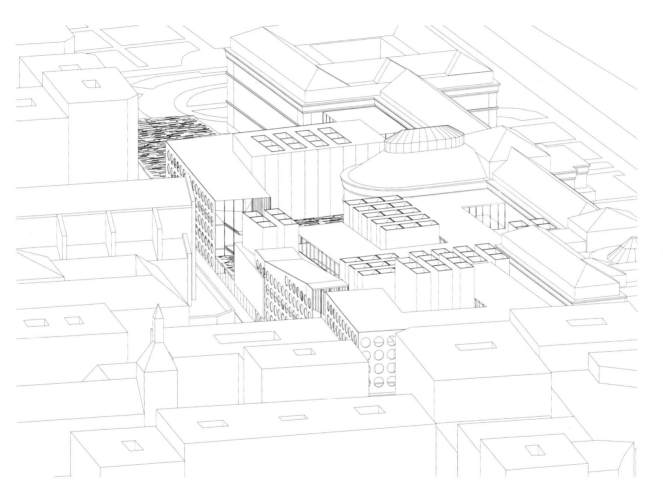

Context view

Aerial view of model

Roof plan montage

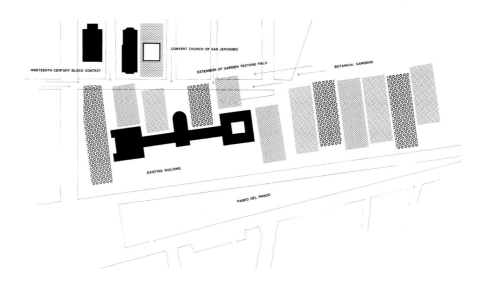

CONVENT CHURCH OF SAN JERONIMO

NINETEENTH CENTURY BLOCK CONTEXT

EXTENSION OF GARDEN TEXTURE FIELD

BOTANICAL GARDENS

EXISTING BUILDING

PASEO DEL PRADO

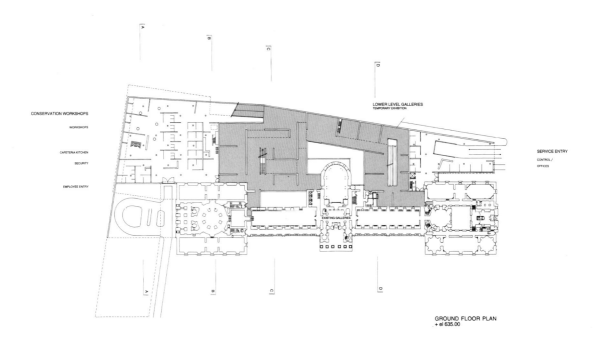

CONSERVATION WORKSHOPS

WORKSHOPS

CAFETERIA KITCHEN

SECURITY

EMPLOYEE ENTRY

LOWER LEVEL GALLERIES
TEMPORARY EXHIBITION

SERVICE ENTRY

CONTROL /

OFFICES

EXISTING GALLERIES

GROUND FLOOR PLAN
+ el 635.00

TOP: Fields Diagram

BOTTOM: Ground-floor plan

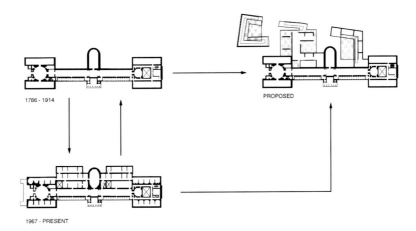

1786 - 1914

PROPOSED

1967 - PRESENT

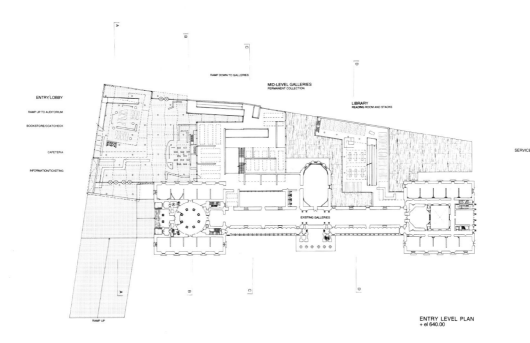

ENTRY/LOBBY

RAMP UP TO AUDITORIUM

BOOKSTORE/COATCHECK

CAFETERIA

INFORMATION/TICKETING

RAMP DOWN TO GALLERIES

MID-LEVEL GALLERIES
PERMANENT COLLECTION

LIBRARY
READING ROOM AND STACKS

SERVICE ENTRY BELOW

EXISTING GALLERIES

RAMP UP

ENTRY LEVEL PLAN
+ el 640.00

TOP: Diagram of extension

BOTTOM: Entry-level plan

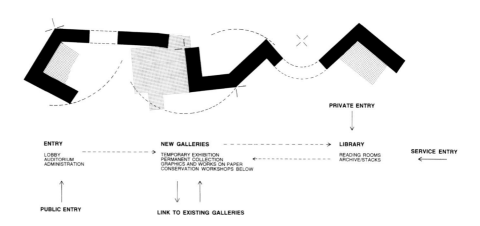

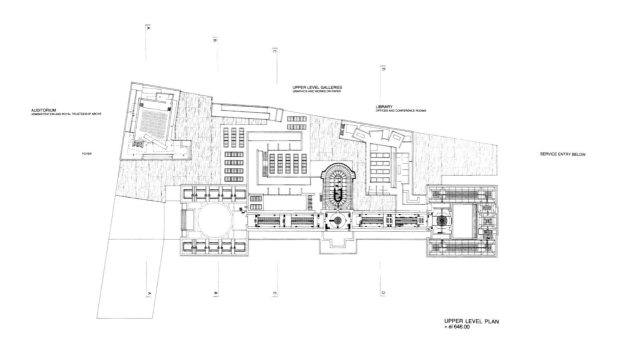

TOP: Program diagram

BOTTOM: Upper-level plan

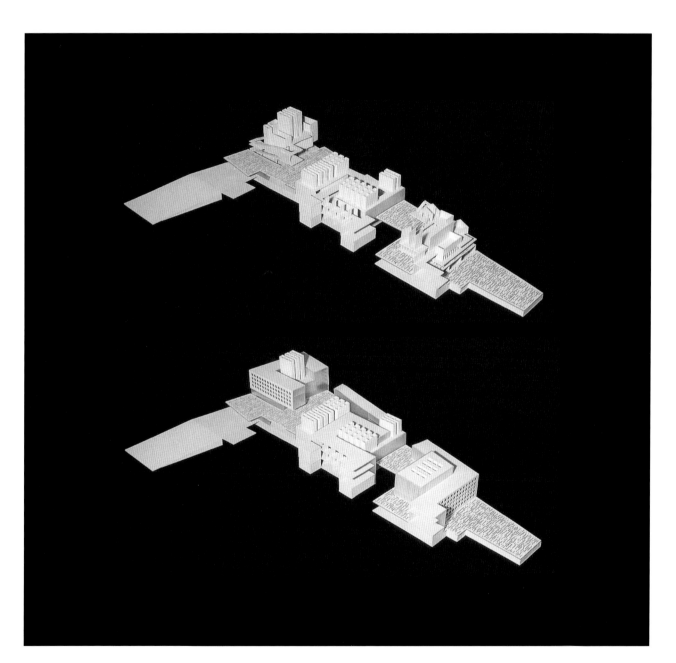

Massing model: program elements and wrappers

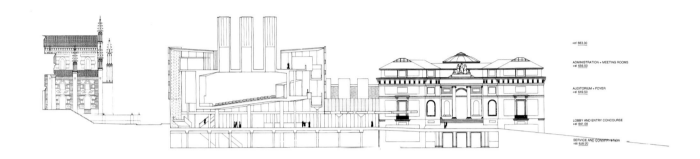

+el 663.00

ADMINISTRATION + MEETING ROOMS
+el 656.50

AUDITORIUM + FOYER
+el 649.50

LOBBY AND ENTRY CONCOURSE
+el 641.00

SERVICE AND CONSERVATION
+el 635.00

CROSS SECTION A-A
ENTRY AND AUDITORIUM

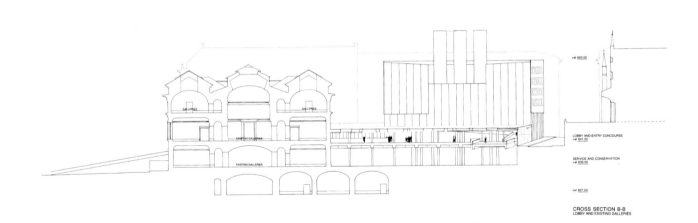

+el 663.00

LOBBY AND ENTRY CONCOURSE
+el 641.00

SERVICE AND CONSERVATION
+el 635.00

+el 627.50

CROSS SECTION B-B
LOBBY AND EXISTING GALLERIES

TOP: Section at auditorium

BOTTOM: Section at entry lobby

TOP: West elevation

BOTTOM: East elevation

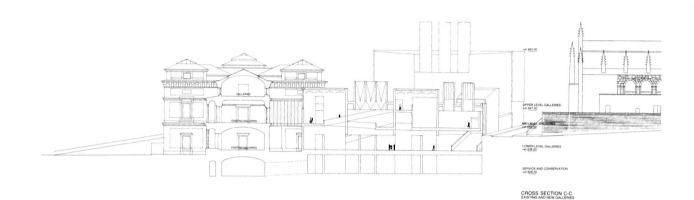

CROSS SECTION C-C
EXISTING AND NEW GALLERIES

UPPER LEVEL GALLERIES
+el 647.00

MID LEVEL GALLERIES
+el 642.50

LOWER LEVEL GALLERIES
+el 636.00

SERVICE AND CONSERVATION
+el 628.00

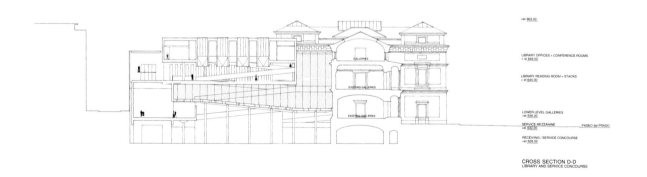

+el 663.00

LIBRARY OFFICES + CONFERENCE ROOMS
+ el 649.50

LIBRARY READING ROOM + STACKS
+ el 644.00

LOWER LEVEL GALLERIES
+el 636.00

SERVICE MEZZANINE   PASEO del PRADO
+el 632.00

RECEIVING / SERVICE CONCOURSE
+el 628.00

CROSS SECTION D-D
LIBRARY AND SERVICE CONCOURSE

TOP: **Section at galleries**

BOTTOM: **Section at library**

Aerial view from Paseo del Prado

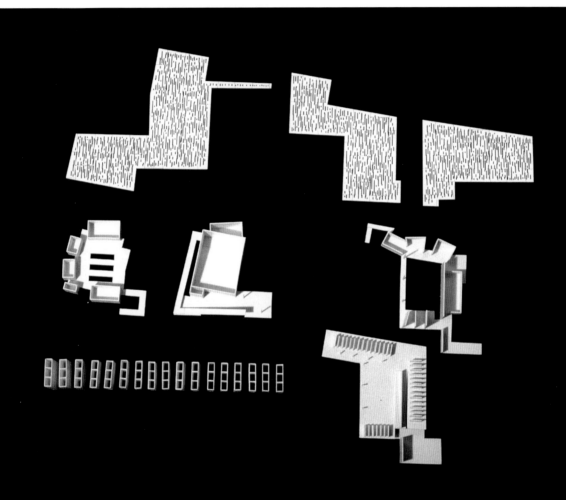

Model elements

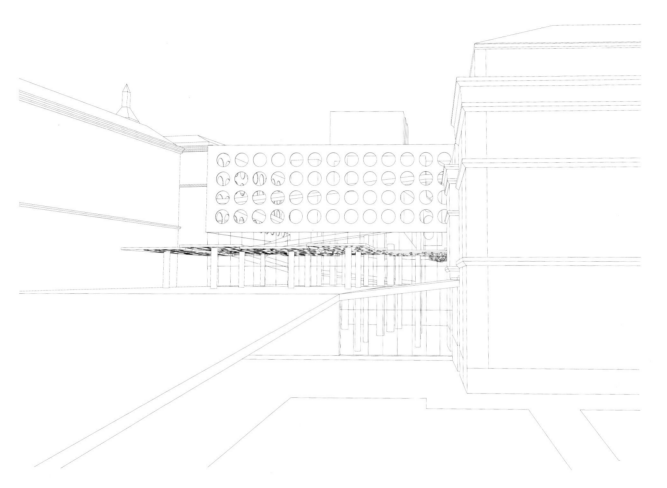

Perspective from Paseo del Prado

Infrastructural

"Think only of essentials: the physics of the gyroscope, the flux of

Urbanism

photons, the architecture of very large structures."   J. G. BALLARD

PROJECTS

Reconstruction of the *Souks* of Beirut, 1994

Logistical Activities Zone, Barcelona, 1996

Avery Computer Studios, New York, 1994. Ceiling detail

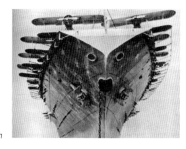

Aircraft Carrier USS *Lexington*

Liner Andrea Doria aground
off Nantucket, 1956

I start with a sequence of three images spanning six decades of the twentieth century:

FIRST IMAGE: the bow of an aircraft carrier, shot from below. The bulk of the craft looms over an invisible horizon, a blank open-mouthed face stares back at the viewer. Published in 1935, in a collection edited by Le Corbusier, the caption reads: "Neptune rises from the sea, crowned with strange garlands, the weapons of Mars."[1] This photograph of the American aircraft carrier *USS* Lexington stands for a moment in which the technical and the aesthetic formed a unified whole. It presents the instrumentality of advanced engineering design and the organization of the forces of production that made construction at this scale possible—processes inescapably linked to the war machine—as fully integrated into a meaningful cultural and aesthetic framework, even to the point of establishing continuity with classical mythology.

SECOND IMAGE: the liner Andrea Doria foundering off the coast of Nantucket in 1956 (taken over twenty years after the first image, still closer in time to the heady world of prewar modernism than to our cynical end-of-century postmodernism). Recalling the iconic status of the liner in the theories of modern architecture, this image could be emblematic of the foundering of the modernist project in the postwar era. By 1956, under the shadow of the Cold War, the modernist dream of an integration of technology and aesthetics was no longer believable. The social and technical forces of modernity were about to become detached from the production of images, both in popular and high culture.

THIRD IMAGE: B-24 bomber factory in Fort Worth, Texas. This aerial view of the factory floor documents the implementation of the modernist dream of rational production under the pressures of the wartime economy: the precise calibration of material, bodies, and time that allowed such incredibly efficient production—"on the front line, and on the production line," as the promotional copy

B-24 Bomber Factory, Fort Worth, Texas, 1944

says. "One B-24 Bomber every four hours": a mechanical ballet performed in this limpid space of production. The space is the exact counterpart to the rational machines produced within it, organized by the infinite perspective of a perfect panoptic transparency, sheltered by the rational tectonics of the factory structure itself. However, it is important to note that this image appears not in its original 1940s context, but in the early 1990s, illustrating an advertisement to raise money for the reconstruction of a *single* B-24 bomber for exhibition purposes. As such, it marks a shift from technologies of production to technologies of reproduction and display. If the factory floor is the ideal space of early modernism, then the museum is the emblematic space postmodernity.

It is this perceived failure of the modernist project that serves to legitimate the subsequent turn toward a postmodern culture of abstract signs and surfaces without depth. In architecture, the consequence of the shift from technologies of production to technologies of reproduction was given expression as an architecture that produced meaning by the grafting of conventional signs onto a neutral technical frame. These images mark a shift from models of formal organization and meaning that work with transparency and depth, to a condition of shallow surfaces, in which meaning resides in graphic information lying on the surface.

But is it not equally plausible to conceive of this shift not as modernism's failure, but as a paradoxical success? Modernity tended toward abstract systems of exchange and serial production. The passage from concrete, material things to ephemeral signs—the dissolution of objects into flows of information—was in many ways already anticipated by the abstract logics of modernity itself. However, the particular form that this transformation takes is not anticipated, nor can it ever be fully controlled from within modernism. Some reassessment is required.

Postmodernism in architecture is usually associated with a rediscovery of architecture's past. However, an equally important shift preceded and in many ways underwrote the postmodern turn to history at the end of the sixties.[2] Postmodernism responded not only to a call to re-inscribe architecture into history, it also responded to a contemporary demand for *meaning* in architecture. History provided a ready-made catalog of "meaningful" forms, but in order for the past to be appropriated and utilized, it had to be detached from its original context and converted into a sign. More than historical reference, it is the presence of this semiotic/structuralist model that identifies postmodernism in architecture. But once architecture's signifying capacity had been opened up, no limit could be placed on signified content. "History" is but one of the many things that a semiotic architecture can signify.

This turn toward a semiotic architecture at the end of the sixties and the beginning of the seventies has itself been subject to intense critical scrutiny—from both a formal and an ideological point of view. But even the most radical critiques have left the fundamental assumption that architecture behaves like a discursive system intact. Deconstruction's radical claim to contest the very possibility of meaning in architecture, for example, was a claim carried out over the territory of meaning and representation, and pays little attention to architecture's instrumentality, or to the complex traffic between representation and materiality. Meaning today may be multiple, contested, contaminated, and partial, but meaning is still the issue.

Nevertheless, an architecture that works exclusively in the semiotic register and defines its role as critique, commentary, or even "interrogation" (laying bare of the intricacies of architecture's complicity with power and politics) has, in some fundamental way,

Intercoastal Waterway, Fort Lauderdale, Florida, 1956–57

given up on the possibility of ever *intervening* in that reality. Under the dominance of the representational model, architecture has surrendered its capacity to imagine, to propose, or to construct alternative realities. As Robin Evans has remarked, a building was once "an opportunity to improve the human condition;" now it is conceived as "an opportunity to express the human condition."[3] Architecture is understood as a discursive system that expresses, critiques, or makes apparent the hard realities of a world that is held safely at arm's length.

One effect of this shift toward images and signs is that architecture's disciplinary frame shifts. It finds itself in competition with other discursive media—painting, film, literature, the Internet, performance art—a field in which architecture often seems to come up short. What these other media lack, of course, is architecture's powerful instrumentality—its capacity not only to critique, but also to actually transform reality. Architecture's relationship to its material is, however, indirect. Unlike activities such as gardening or woodworking, where something concrete is made by direct contact

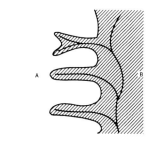

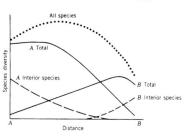

with the material, the architect (like the engineer, the urbanist, or the ecologist) operates on reality at a distance, and through the mediation of abstract systems such as notation, projection, or calculation. Indirect contact is the necessary counterpart to the larger scale of intervention. Architecture works simultaneously with abstract images and with material realities, in complex interplay. It is a *material* practice .

It is not entirely coincidental that the twenty-five year period coinciding with the rise of postmodernism in architecture has seen a massive defunding of urban infrastructure. In the United States, public investment in civic works—highways, railroads, water supply and control, land reclamation, mass transit—is at an all time low. While architects cannot logically be held accountable for these complex political and economical shifts, it might be argued that by the production of a theoretical framework to justify an architecture of surface and sign, architects have, consciously or not, participated in their own marginalization. If architects assert that signs and information are more important than infrastructure, why would bureaucrats or politicians disagree? As much as they have been excluded from the development of the city, architects themselves have retreated from questions of function, implementation, technique, finance, and material practice. And while architects are relatively powerless to provoke the changes necessary to generate renewed investment in infrastructure, they *can* begin to redirect their own imaginative and technical efforts toward the questions of infrastructure. A toolbox of new and existing procedures can be

51

expanded by reference to architecture's traditional alliance with territorial organization and functionality.

This is the context within which I want to situate the shift in recent practice toward infrastructure. Going beyond stylistic or formal issues, infrastructural urbanism offers a new model for practice and a renewed sense of architecture's potential to structure the future of the city. Infrastructural urbanism understands architecture as *material* practice—as an activity that works in and among the world of things, and not exclusively with meaning and image. It is an architecture dedicated to concrete proposals and realistic strategies of implementation and not distanced commentary or critique. It is a way of working at the large scale that escapes suspect notions of master planning and the heroic ego of the individual architect. Infrastructural urbanism marks a return to instrumentality and a move away from the representational imperative in architecture.

This does not imply a simple return to the now discredited certainties of modernism. Two claims can be made: first, that architecture's instrumentality can be reconceived—not as a mark of modernity's demand for efficient implementation but as the site of architecture's contact with the complexity of the real. By immersing architecture in the world of things, it becomes possible to produce what Robin Evans, paraphrasing Lyotard, has referred to as a "volatile, unordered, unpoliceable communication that will always outwit the judicial domination of language."[4] The second claim is for a practice engaged in time and process—a practice not devoted to the production of autonomous objects, but rather to the production of directed fields in which program, event, and activity can play themselves out.

In an interview conducted fifteen years ago, Michel Foucault noted that "Architects are not the engineers or technicians of the three great variables: territory, communication and speed."[5] While it is hard to argue Foucault's point as an assessment of the current condition, it deserves to be pointed out that historically this has not been the case. Land surveying, territorial organization, local ecologies, road construction, shipbuilding, hydraulics, fortification, bridge building, war machines, and networks of communication and transportation were all part of the traditional competence of the architect before the rise of disciplinary specialization. Territory, communication, and speed are properly *infrastructural* problems, and architecture as a discipline has developed specific technical means to deal effectively with these variables. Mapping, projection, calculation, notation, and visualization are among architecture's traditional tools for operating at the very large scale. These procedures can be reclaimed for architecture, and supplemented with new technologies of design and simulation now available.

But rethinking infrastructure is only one aspect of a larger move away from the representational model, one of the many implications of architecture understood as a *material practice*. Material practices (ecology or engineering for example) are concerned with the behavior of large scale assemblages over time. They do not work primarily with images or meaning, or even with

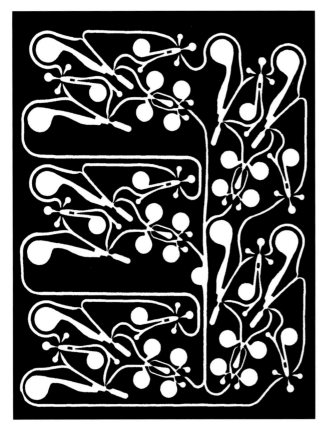

Computer flow diagram

objects, but with *performance*: energy inputs and outputs, the calibration of force and resistance. They are less concerned with what things look like and more concerned with what they can do. Although these material practices work instrumentally, they are not limited to the direct manipulation of given material. Instead they project transformations of reality by means of abstract techniques such as notation, simulation, or calculation. Material practices organize and transform aggregates of labor, materials, energy and resources, but they work through necessarily mediated procedures—operations of drawing and projection, for example—that leave their trace on the work. Material practices deploy an open catalog of techniques without preconceived formal ends .

In architecture and urbanism, technique does not belong to an individual but to the discipline as a whole. As Foucault has reminded us, techniques are social before they are technical. Hence, to think of architecture as a material practice does not mean leaving questions of meaning entirely behind. Architecture works with cultural and social variables as well as with physical materials, and architecture's capacity to signify is one tool available to the architect working in the city. But material practices do not attempt to control or predetermine meaning. Instead, they go beyond the paradoxes of the linguistic to examine the effects of signifying practices on performance and behavior. Material practices are not about expression—expressing either the point of view of an author or of the collective will of a society; rather they condense, transform, and materialize concepts.[6]

53

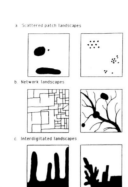

a. Scattered patch landscapes

b. Network landscapes

c. Interdigitated landscapes

d. Checkerboard landscapes

RIGHT: Richard T. T. Foreman, landscape ecology diagrams

BELOW: Carquinez Bridge Approach, Crockett, California, 1958

54

Architecture is uniquely capable of structuring the city in ways not available to practices such as literature, film, politics, installation art, or advertising. Yet because of its capacity to actualize social and cultural concepts, it can also contribute something that strictly technical disciplines such as engineering cannot. When Walter Benjamin writes that "construction fulfills the role of the unconscious," he articulates the capacity of certain structures to act as a scaffold for a complex series of events not anticipated by the architect—meanings and affects existing outside of the control of a single author that continuously evolve over time.

SEVEN PROPOSITIONS

In retrospect, I really think that we are now dealing with the same issues again, after the "semantic nightmare."

REM KOOLHAAS, 1991

1. Infrastructure works not so much to propose specific buildings on given sites, but to construct the site itself. Infrastructure prepares the ground for future building and creates the conditions for future events. Its primary modes of operation are: the division, allocation, and construction of surfaces; the provision of services to support future programs; and the establishment of networks for movement, communication, and exchange. Infrastructure's medium is geography.

2. Infrastructures are flexible and anticipatory. They work with time and are open to change. By specifying what must be fixed and what is subject to change, they can be precise and indeterminate at the same time. They work through management and cultivation, changing slowly to adjust to shifting conditions. They do not progress toward a predetermined state (as with master planning strategies), but are always evolving within a loose envelope of constraints.

3. Infrastructural work recognizes the collective nature of the city and allows for the participation of multiple authors. Infrastructures give direction to future work in the city not by the establishment of rules or codes (top-down), but by fixing points of service, access, and structure (bottom-up). Infrastructure creates a directed field where different architects and designers can contribute, but it sets technical and instrumental limits to their work. Infrastructure itself works strategically, but it encourages tactical improvisation. Infrastructural work moves away from self referentiality and individual expression toward collective enunciation.

4. Infrastructures accommodate local contingency while maintaining overall continuity. In the design of highways, bridges, canals, or aqueducts, for example, an extensive catalog of strategies exist to accommodate irregularities in the terrain (doglegs, viaducts, cloverleaves, switchbacks, etc.), which are creatively employed to accommodate existing conditions while maintaining functional continuity. Nevertheless, infrastructure's default condition is regularity—in the desert, the highway runs straight. Infrastructures are above all pragmatic. Because it operates instrumentally, infrastructural design is indifferent to formal debates. Invested neither in (ideal) regularity nor in (disjunctive) irregularity, the designer is free to employ whatever works given any particular condition.

5. Although static in and of themselves, infrastructures organize and manage complex systems of flow, movement, and exchange. Not only do they provide a network of pathways, they also work through systems of locks, gates, and valves—a series of checks that control and regulate flow. It is therefore a mistake to think that infrastructures can in a utopian way enable new freedoms, that there is a possibility of a net gain through new networks. What seems crucial is the degree of play designed into the system, slots left unoccupied, space left free for unanticipated development. This also opens the question of the formal description of infrastructural systems: infrastructures tend to be hierarchical and tree-like. However, there are effects of scale (a capillary effect when the elements get very numerous and very small) and effects of synergy (when systems overlap and interchange), both of which tend to produce field conditions that disrupt the overall tendency of infrastructural systems to organize themselves in linear fashion.

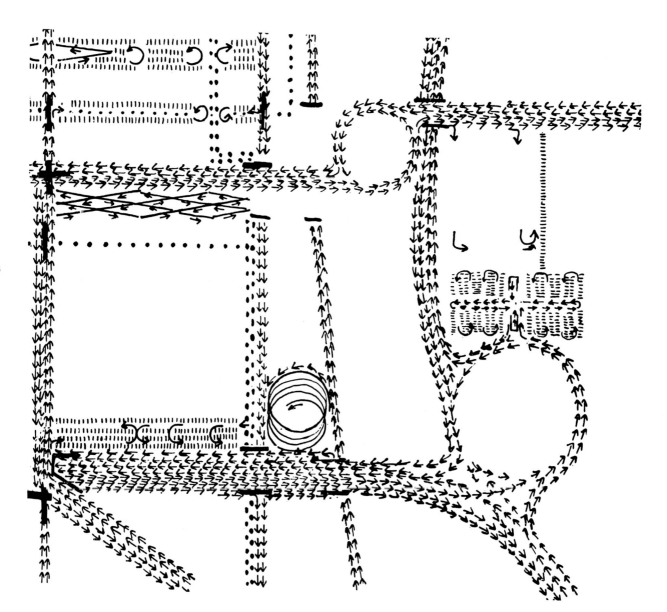

Louis Kahn: movement diagrams, Philadelphia Planning Study.

6. Infrastructural systems work like artificial ecologies. They manage the flows of energy and resources on a site, and they direct the density and distribution of a habitat. They create the conditions necessary to respond to incremental adjustments in resource availability, and modify the status of inhabitation in response to changing environmental conditions.

7. Infrastructures allow detailed design of typical elements or repetitive structures, facilitating an architectural approach to urbanism. Instead of moving always down in scale from the general to the specific, infrastructural design begins with the precise delineation of specific architectural elements within specific limits. Unlike other models (planning codes or typological norms for example) that tend to schematize and regulate architectural form and work by prohibition, the limits to architectural design in infrastructural complexes are technical and instrumental. In infrastructural urbanism, form matters, but more for what it can do than for what it looks like.

"The time has come to approach architecture urbanistically and urbanism architecturally"[7]

NOTES:
1. Le Corbusier, *Aircraft* (1935; reprint New York: Universe Books, 1988), illustration 18.
2. Robert Venturi, *Complexity and Contradiction in Architecture* (New York: The Museum of Modern Art, 1966); Colin Rowe and Fred Koetter, *Collage City* (Cambridge, MA: MIT Press, 1978). Note that the text to *Collage City* was completed in 1973 and widely circulated before the publication of the book.
3. "Words like investigation, enquiry and interrogation, used much in describing what designers do, suggest that designing is a way of finding out, as if the process of design were conducted in some kind of mental laboratory in which the boundaries of knowledge were being pushed slowly but surely forward." Robin Evans, "Bad News," paper delivered at th Conference on Theory and Practice in the Work of John Hedjuk, Canadian Centre of Architecture, Montreal, 15 May 1992.
4. Robin Evans, The Projective Cast (Cambridge, MA: MIT Press, 1995), 91–2.
5. Michel Foucault, "Space, Knowledge, and Power," in *The Foucault Reader,* ed. Paul Rabinow (New York: Pantheon Books, 1984), 244.
6. In the terms of the distinction proposed by Gilles Deleuze, material practices are more concerned with the actualization of the virtual than with the realization of the possible. See Gilles Deleuze, *Bergsonism,* trans. Hugh Tomlinson and Barbara Habberjam (New York: Zone Books, 1989), 97. On the subject of virtuality, and on a number of other points, I have referred to Michael Speaks, "Redirecting the Global Space of Flows," paper given at the Berlage Institute, Amsterdam, 28 October 1997.
7. Alison Smithson, ed., *Team 10 Primer* (Cambridge, MA: MIT Press, 1968), 73. While an entire section of the *Primer* is devoted to "Urban Infrastructure," the primary subject is the problem of large-scale motorways. Nevertheless, Team 10's attention to questions of scale, use, movement and flow, and the evolution of the urban landscape over time make their thoughts an exemplary and obligatory starting point in any discussion of architecture and infrastructure.

57

The Reconstruction of the *Souks* of Beirut

COMPETITION PROJECT, 1994
ARCHITECT: Stan Allen
ASSISTED BY: Jack Phillips and Katherine Kim

When reconstructing a city that has grown slowly over time to encompass the architectures of many cultures, it is imperative to recognize the passage of time and to accept the partial and incomplete nature of the planning process itself. Precise understanding of the city's architecture is required, but it is also important to recognize the intrinsic limits of design operations. A city culture as complex as Beirut's cannot be recreated overnight on the basis of a single "masterplan." How can one impose a measure of unity while respecting the essential diversity of the city to come?

We propose four distinct but interrelated operations:

1. To preserve and reconstruct as many of the existing historic structures as possible, accepting all of the limitations and irregularities that this might impose.

2. To recover the ground of the site with a series of continuous surfaces.

3. To construct a series of new buildings to accommodate a variety of functions: markets, restaurants, offices, residences, cinemas, and department stores.

RIGHT: Riccardo Morandi, Parco del Valentino Hall, 1959

OPPOSITE: Roof construction

LEFT: Typical *souk* street (pre-Civil War)

BELOW: Konstantin Melnikov, Sukhareva Market, 1924

4. Finally, and perhaps most importantly, to construct a vast roof of steel and glass extending across the site, stitching together a previously fragmented context.

This is a fundamentally architectural approach, concentrating the design effort at the level of the urban infrastructure. Unity is achieved by the continuous rhythm of the roof structure, while the diversity of city life is cultivated below. It should be noted that while preliminary proposals for the *souks* and the other buildings have been submitted, a major advantage of this scheme is that it anticipates the future incorporation of various styles and various functions within an overall framework. It allows phasing, incremental realization, and broad participation in the reconstruction process. It is an optimistic approach, confident that the will to rebuild is strong enough to accommodate the complexity of the city to come.

59

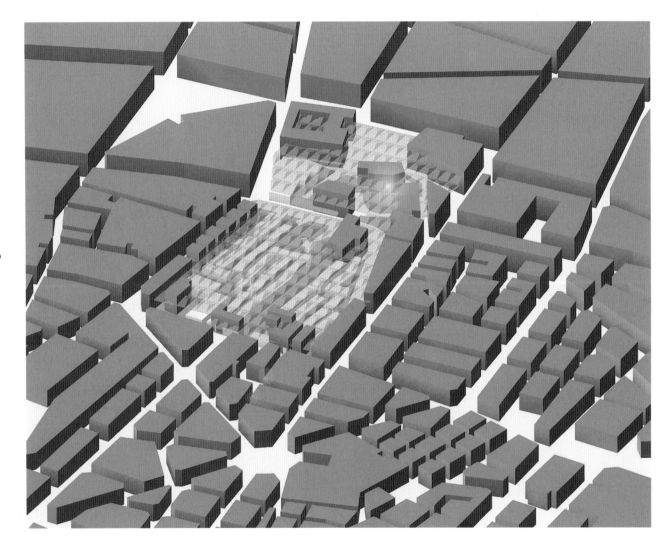

Context view

Site plan

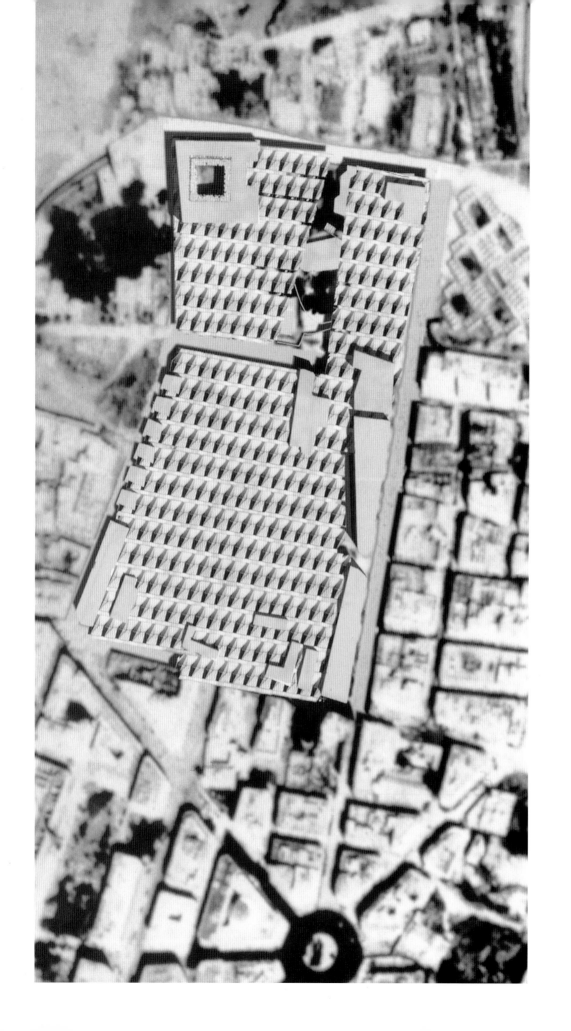

ABOVE: *Souk* layout

OPPOSITE: Montage: roof plan in context

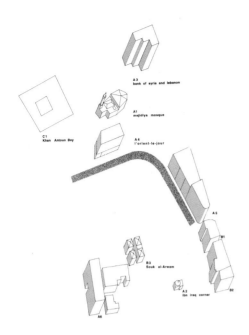

Existing structures

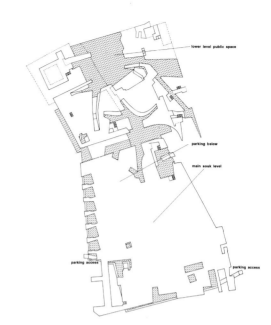

New surfaces

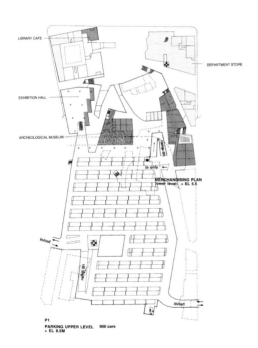

Program: lower level

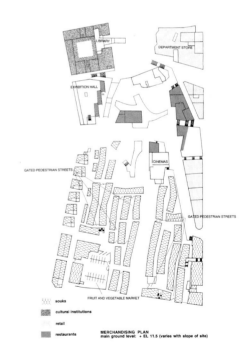

Program: main level

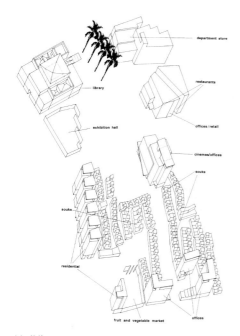

Proposed buildings

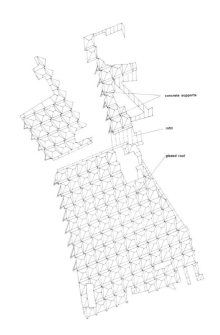

Roof

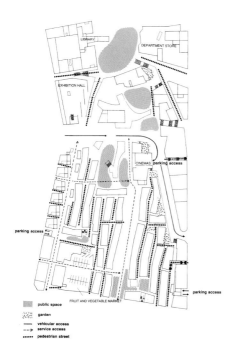

Public spaces

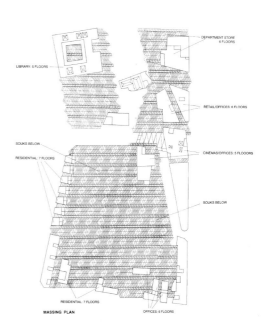

Interstitial spaces

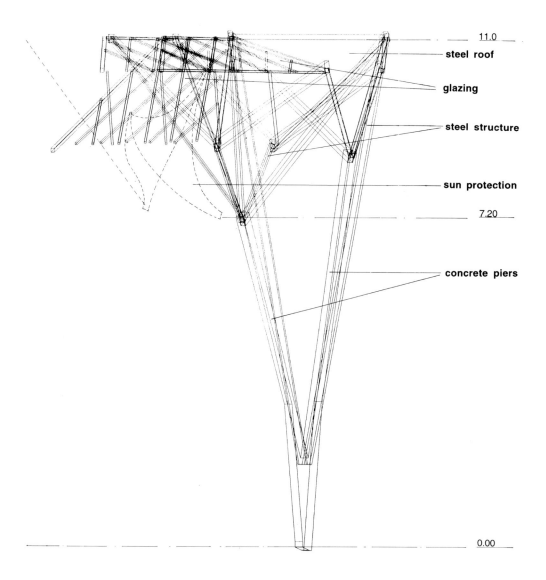

66

11.0

steel roof

glazing

steel structure

sun protection

7.20

concrete piers

0.00

35.5
29.5
22.5
15
5.5
00

AVENUE DES FRANÇAIS

TRABLOUS STREET

DEPARTMENT STORE BEYOND

RESTORED CITY WALL

MAJIDIYA MOSQUE

L'ORIENT-LE JOUR BUILDING

SKYLIGH

68

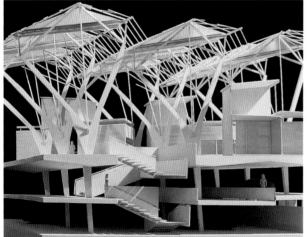

TOP: Long section

BOTTOM: Section model

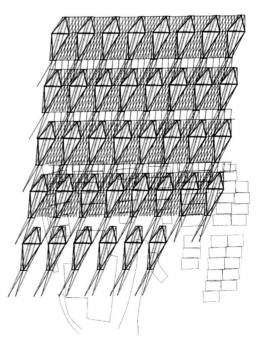

BOTTOM: Roof modules

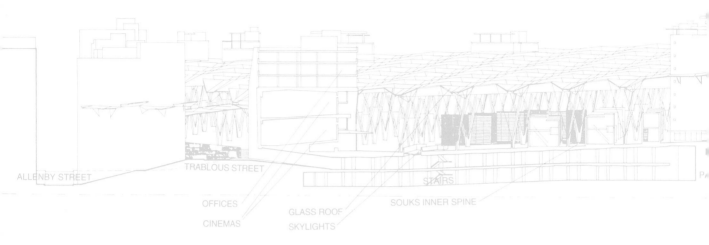

ALLENBY STREET   TRABLOUS STREET   STAIRS   PA

                  OFFICES   SOUKS INNER SPINE

                  CINEMAS   GLASS ROOF
                                 SKYLIGHTS

70

TOP: **Cross-section**

BOTTOM: **Study model**

OPPOSITE: **Section model**

Logistical Activities Zone, Barcelona

COMPETITION, 1996

ARCHITECT: Stan Allen

ASSISTED BY: Céline Parmentier, Tsuto Sakamoto,
Adriana Nacheva, and Troels Rugbjerg

User's Manual research and layout by Nona Yehia

The municipality of Barcelona intends to divert the LLobregat River and extend its existing port facilities. An open international competition was held in 1996 for the Logistical Activities Zone (ZAL) adjacent to the new port area. We took this competition as an opportunity to examine the potentials of an infrastructural urbanism. Our design strategy consisted of setting down the traces of an architectural infrastructure that would allow flexible development while maintaining unified identity: a directed field within which the future life of the site could unfold; an architectural means to impose minimal although precise limits on future construction.

Refusing the chaos of the suburban landscape without resorting to nostalgic urban patterns, we sought an order specific to the open zones at the edge of the city. Two prototypical strategies were proposed: a division of land that recognizes the presence of nature and maintains open green space; a continuous architectural infrastructure that will allow flexible development while maintaining unified identity.

Although developed initially by means of conventional representational techniques (plans, sections, and models) the elaboration of the project required new representational strategies. The diagrams, maps, scores, and scripts that anticipate the event structure of the site over time have been compiled into a *User's Manual*. In the infrastructural approach, limits to future development are set materially, and not through codes, zoning, or bureaucratic limits. Hence, the role of the notational schemas collected here is not to set limits but to imagine multiple program scenarios and to

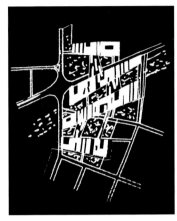

LEFT: Sketch of structure

OPPOSITE: Model: infrastructural roof

73

chart their interaction. These notations do not so much map an exact correspondence between architecture and activity as articulate a degree of play between form and event, a loose fit of organization and program.

1. SURFACES

Borrowing a concept from landscape ecology, the given surface area of the site is organized into *patches* and *corridors*. *Patches* are defined as nonlinear surface areas—in this case either green areas where a return to indigenous habitat is encouraged or built-up areas to accommodate the new programs.[1] *Corridors* are infrastructural pathways containing movement, services, and function. The superposition of these two systems creates a mosaic of natural and artificial surfaces.

2. MOVEMENT

Boundary and through roads are connected into the present system of urban circulation. To facilitate connection with the ZAL, the primary circulation is on uninterrupted east-west routes. Secondary circulation is by means of local connecting roads aligned with the disjunctive network of patches. Pedestrian movement is at an upper level within the depths of trusses supporting a continuous roof structure.

3. PROGRAM

Four broad programmatic categories are proposed: *work* (workshops and ateliers for artists and artisans); *display* (showrooms and other exhibition facilities), *service* (vehicle services, hotel and office space); and *recreation* (sports facilities and open green spaces for leisure and events). Individual patches are programmed in relation to access, adjacency, and proximity to services.

4. PATCH TYPOLOGIES

Instead of specific design proposals for future occupation of the site, a series of loose organizational typologies are proposed. Depending on density and organization, patches might function as habitat, barrier, filter, source, or sink for future activity. Scale and density of architectural occupation in turn suggests possible programs.

5. INFRASTRUCTURE

The architectural space of the patches is articulated by a continuous roof structure supported on a regular grid of thin steel

LEFT: View of existing site

OPPOSITE: Plan: montage of scenarios

columns. This infrastructural element is adaptable and flexible. A lightweight fabric covering can be added to shelter public spaces or outdoor service areas, and where buildings are proposed it can be integrated into the structural system as sunbreak or service space.

Taking an optimistic view of the future of the site, this project anticipates the participation of different architects, agencies, and individuals in the construction of the site. It seeks to establish a realistic framework within which these collective contributions can be organized and coordinated. Working not with the bureaucratic tools of zoning—regulations or codes—it seeks to establish precise technical and instrumental limits to future construction. By creating a structured field condition that is architecturally specific yet programatically indeterminate, the future life of the site is free to unfold beyond the fixed limits of a masterplan.

NOTES

1. "We may define *patch* as a non-linear surface area differing in appearance from its surroundings....Patches are often embedded in a *matrix*, a surrounding area that has a different species, structure, or occupation." Richard T. T. Forman and Michael Godron, *Landscape Ecology* (New York: Wiley, 1986), 83.

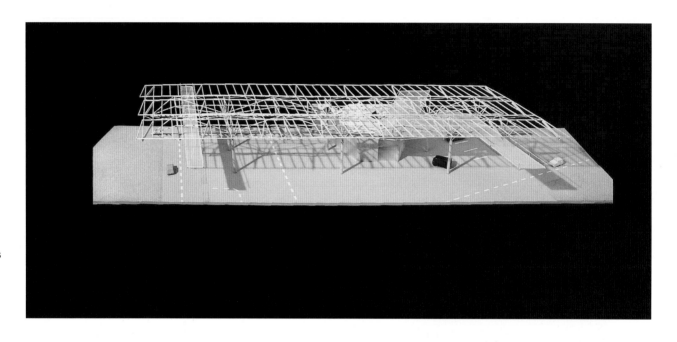

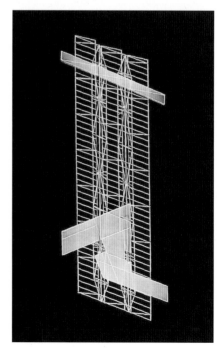

ABOVE: **Partial model**

RIGHT: **Roof from below**

OPPOSITE AND FOLLOWING PAGES: *User's Manual*

barcelona manual

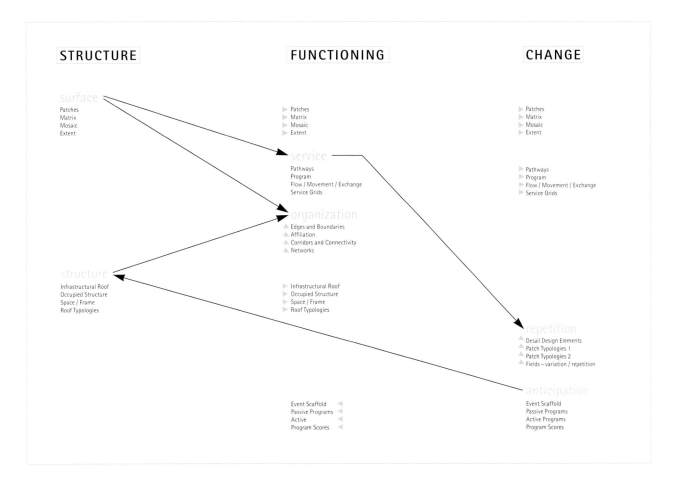

STRUCTURE

FUNCTIONING

CHANGE

surface

Patches
Matrix
Mosaic
Extent

Patches
Matrix
Mosaic
Extent

Patches
Matrix
Mosaic
Extent

service

Pathways
Program
Flow / Movement / Exchange
Service Grids

Pathways
Program
Flow / Movement / Exchange
Service Grids

organization

Edges and Boundaries
Affiliation
Corridors and Connectivity
Networks

structure

Infrastructural Roof
Occupied Structure
Space / Frame
Roof Typologies

Infrastructural Roof
Occupied Structure
Space / Frame
Roof Typologies

repetition

Detail Design Elements
Patch Typologies 1
Patch Typologies 2
Fields – variation / repetition

anticipation

Event Scaffold
Passive Programs
Active
Program Scores

Event Scaffold
Passive Programs
Active Programs
Program Scores

	1B	1C	1D	SURFACE
2A	2B	2C	2D	SERVICE
3A	3B	3C	3D	ORGANIZATION
4A	4B	4C	4D	STRUCTURE
5A	5B	5C	5D	REPETITION
6A	6B	6C	6D	ANTICIPATION

1A
SURFACE
PATCHES

a. Scattered patch landscapes

b. Network landscapes

c. Interdigitated landscapes

d. Checkerboard landscapes

RICHARD T.T. FORMAN
PATCH TYPOLOGIES

a nonlinear surface area differing in appearance from its surroundings.
the density of patches, or the fineness of a mosaic.
an area that has been disturbed within a matrix.
the rate of appearance and disappearance of patches.
an area caused by an animal social behavior or by low-intensity, short lived fluctuations in environmental factors within a matrix.

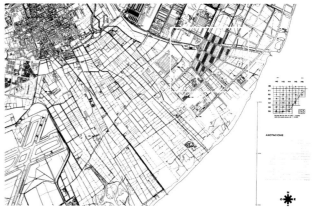

LOCATION PLAN

1. Infrastructure works not so much to propose specific buildings on given sites, but to construct the site itself. Infrastructure prepares the ground for future building, and creates the conditions for future events. Its primary modes of operation are:

1. The division, allocation and construction of **surfaces**
2. The provision of **services** to support future programs
3. The establishment of **networks** for movement, communication and exchange

Infrastructure's medium is geography.

1A		1C	1D	SURFACE
2A	2B	2C	2D	SERVICE
3A	3B	3C	3D	ORGANIZATION
4A	4B	4C	4D	STRUCTURE
5A	5B	5C	5D	REPETITION
6A	6B	6C	6D	ANTICIPATION

1B
SURFACE
MATRIX

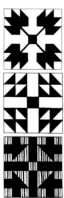

QUILTING PATTERNS

GREEN MATRIX

PATCHES + CORRIDORS

an area that becomes free of disturbance within a chronically disturbed matrix
the rate of appearance and disappearance of patches.
a table of replacement rates over a time period for all landscape elements present
a landscape with a densely built-up matrix.

78

1C
SURFACE
MOSAIC

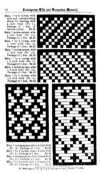

FROEBEL PATTERNS

PLAN DETAILS / PROGRAM SCENARIOS
EVENT FIELD

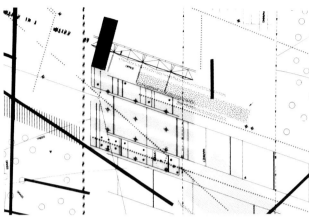

PLAN DETAILS / PROGRAM SCENARIOS
OFFICE PATCH / GREEN SPACE

a tract of patches of different aged trees.
a system exhibiting a pattern of long-term change along with short-term internal spatial conversions.
a state of being in equilibrium (oscillating around a central position), but susceptible to being diverted to another equilibrium.
methods that concurrently analyze many factors, plus the relationship among factors.

HILBERSEIMER
SITE PLAN OF HYDE PARK

1D
SURFACE
EXTENT

OVERVIEW OF SITE

a pattern where species distributions are related to the width of a landscape element.
the establishment, and usually defense, of a certain small area ("territory") against intrusions by other individuals of the same species.
a map that accurately represents a spatial ordering, but is not proportional to the distance and the length of time necessary to cover a route. Also, a geometry dealing with the continuous connectedness between points of a figure.

URBAN CONTEXT DIAGRAM

2A
SERVICE
PATHWAYS

NOTATIONS:
Traditional representations presume stable objects and fixed subjects. But the contemporary city is not reducible to an artifact. The city is a place where visible and invisible streams of information, capital and subjects, interact in complex formations. They form a dispersed fireld, a network of flows. In order to describe or to intervene in this new field we need representational techniques that engage time and change, shifting scales, mobile points of view and multiple programs. In order to map this complexity, some measure of control may have to be relinquished. To open architectural representation to the score, the map, the diagram and the script could establish a basis for exchange with other disciplines such as film, music and performance. The score allows for the simultaneous presentation and interplay of information in diverse scales, on shifting coordinates and even of differing linguistic codes. The script allows the designer to engage program, event and time on specifically architectural terms. New maps and diagrams might begin to suggest new ways of working with the complex dynamics of the contemporary city.

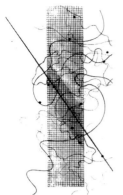

JOHN CAGE'S SCORE FOR FONTANA MIX

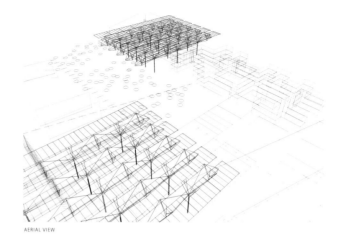

AERIAL VIEW

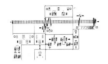

SCORE FOR STOCKHAUSEN'S ZYKLUS

the degree to which circuit loops in a network are present.
the combination of network connectivity and circuitry.
the degree to which all nodes in a system are linked by corridors.

2. **Infrastructural** work recognizes the collective nature of the city, and allows for the participation of multiple authors. Infrastructures give direction to future work in the city not by the establishment of rules or codes (top-down), but by fixing points of service, access and structure (bottom-up). Infrastructure creates a directional field, where different architects and designers can contribute, but it sets technical and instrumental limits to their work. Infrastructure itself works strategically, but it encourages tactical improvisation.

80

2B
SERVICE
PROGRAM

MARKET SERVICES

PROGRAM PATCHES

a measure of how many comparable examples of a characteristic exist at different levels of scale, from the local to the global.
the ability of a system, when subjected to an environmental change or potential disturbance, to withstand or resist variation.

ERECTING SHOP

2C
SERVICE
FLOW / MOVEMENT / EXCHANGE

MODEL DETAIL

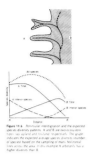

Figure 11.6 *Peninsular interdigitation and the expected species diversity patterns. A and B are two ecosystem types- say upland and lowland respectively. The graph indicates the expected average species diversity (number of species) based on the sampling of mass horizontal lines across the area. In this example A arbitrarily has a higher diversity than B.*

RAILWAY INTERCHANGE

KAHN FLOW DIAGRAM

2. Although static in and of themselves, **infrastructures** organize and manage complex systems of flow, movement and exchange. Not only do they provide a network of pathways, thye also work through systems of locks, gates and valves - a series of checks that control and regulate flow.

81

2D
SERVICE
SERVICE GRIDS

a process by which objects leave one area and spread to another area.
a process by which objects extend their area of coverage while continuing to occupy the original position.
an event or characteristic that has a direct or relatively direct effect on an organism.

PEDESTRIAN WALKWAY

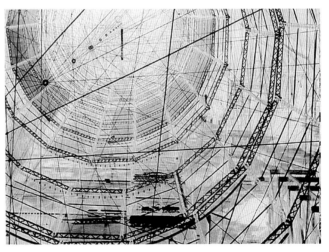

3A
ORGANIZATION
EDGES + BOUNDARIES

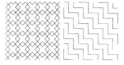

QUILTING PATTERNS

9. Crystal pattern;
from Johann Killian,
Der Kristall (Berlin:
P. Zsolnay, 1937), p.
142, ill. 33. Photo
courtesy of Ludwig
Mies van der Rohe

Figure 9.1 Polygon numbering

AERIAL PHOTOGRAPH OF SITE

a distinctive species composition or relative
abundance in the outer band of a patch (i.e., different from the species composition or relative abundance of the patch interior).
the degree of abruptness
between landscape elements.
the effect of the edge on flows,
analogous to a semipermeable membrane.

3. Infrastructures accomodate local contigency while maintaining overall continuity. In the design of highways, bridges, canals or aqueducts, for example, an extensive catalogue of strategies exist to accomodate irregularities in the terrain (doglegs, viaducts, cloverleaves, switchbacks, etc.) which are creatively employed to accomodate existing conditions while maintaining functional continuity. Infrasructure's default condition is regularity - in the desert, the highway runs straight. Infrastructures are above all pragmatic. Because it operates instrumentally, infrastructural design is indifferent to formal debates. Invested neither in (ideal) regularity or in (disjunctive) irregularity, the designer is free to employ whatever works in the particular conditions.

82

3B
ORGANIZATION
AFFILIATION

PERFORMANCE:
This project marks a shift away from issues of representation to engage architecture as a MATERIAL PRACTICE.
Material practices, (ecology, or engineering for example) do not work primarily with images or meaning but
with PERFORMANCE: energy inputs and outputs, the calibration of force and resistance. They are less concerned
with what things look like and more concerned with
what they can do. Material practices do not attempt to
control or predetermine meaning. Instead, they go
beyond the paradoxes of the linguistic to examine the
effects of signifying practices on performance and
behavior. Although these material practices work
instrumentally, they are not limited to the direct manipulation of given material. Instead they project transformations of reality by means of abstract techniques such
as notation, simulation or calculation.

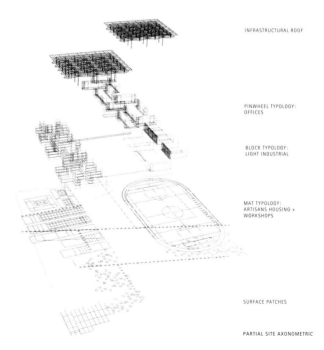

INFRASTRUCTURAL ROOF

PINWHEEL TYPOLOGY:
OFFICES

BLOCK TYPOLOGY:
LIGHT INDUSTRIAL

MAT TYPOLOGY:
ARTISANS HOUSING +
WORKSHOPS

SURFACE PATCHES

PARTIAL SITE AXONOMETRIC

DECENTRALIZATION DIAGRAM

DRAINAGE DENSITIES

layers or streams of air moving in parallel fashion, one on top of another.
a location where three or more types
of landscape elements intersect.
a line corridor seperating two types of
landscape elements, thus providing three types in
close proximity.

QUILTING PATTERNS

3C
ORGANIZATION
CORRIDORS + CONNECTIVITY

PAVED SURFACES

MOVEMENT NOTATION

STITCH MAP

a wide band with a central interior environment that contains an abundance of interior species.
ecological conditions being modified significantly by the presence of an interconnection of corridors.
a narrow band essentially dominated throughout by edge species.
a narrow strip of land that differs from the matrix on either side.
selective absorption or blocking that prevents objects from crossing a corridor.

Figure 11.2 Effect of corridor width and breaks on movement across a landscape. The shaded areas indicate conditions, emphasis on movement and emphasize the critical importance of break areas (from Forman, 1981. Courtesy of Ecology). CSBR I

3D
ORGANIZATION
NETWORK

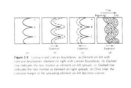

Figure 5.9 Concave and convex boundaries. (a) Element on left with concave boundaries, element on right with convex boundaries. (b) Dashed line indicates the new frontier as element on left spreads. (c) Dashed line indicates the new frontier as element on right spreads. (d) Over time, the concave margin or the spreading element on left becomes convex.

Figure 11.12 Two networks in topological space that differ in both connectivity and circuitry. Simple indices are given in the text for evaluating the amount of both variables that together are a measure of network complexity. Network b represents the dotted area of map c, indicating hedgerows of a medieval field pattern in Devon, England. This form of late Saxon origin is shown in the Domesday Book of 1086, probably as pastureland. The characteristic small and irregular fields were created in the following century (adapted from Hoskins, 1955).

SITE NETWORKS

the degree to which circuit loops in a network are present.
the combination of network connectivity and circuitry.
the degree to which all nodes in a system are linked by corridors.

Figure 4.2 TWO NETWORK CATEGORIES: 'BRANCHING NETWORKS' (A) WITHOUT CLOSED LOOPS AND 'CIRCUIT NETWORKS' (B) WITH CLOSED LOOPS

4. Formal description of **infrastructural systems:** infrastructures tend to be hierarchical and tree-like, however there are effects of scale - a capillary effect when the elements get very numerous and very small - and the effects of synergy, when systems overlap and interchange, both of which tend to produce field conditions that work against an exclusively vectorial organization of infrastructural systems.

1A	1B	1C	1D	SURFACE
2A	2B	2C	2D	SERVICE
3A	3B	3C	3D	ORGANIZATION
	4B	4C	4D	STRUCTURE
5A	5B	5C	5D	REPETITION
6A	6B	6C	6D	ANTICIPATION

4A
STRUCTURE
INFRASTRUCTURAL ROOF

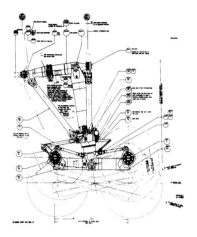

a structure composed of linear features that interconnect and form circuits or loops.
a threshold above which a force destroys a system.
the intensities, frequencies, and types of perturbations (disturbances) characterizing each ecosystem type in a cluster of ecosystem types.

4. **Infrastructural** systems work like artificial ecologies. They manage the flows of energy and resources on a site, and direct the density and distribution of habitat. They create the conditions necessary to respond to incremental adjustments in resource availability, and modify status of inhabitation in response to changing environmental conditions.

84

1A	1B	1C	1D	SURFACE
2A	2B	2C	2D	SERVICE
3A	3B	3C	3D	ORGANIZATION
4A		4C	4D	STRUCTURE
5A	5B	5C	5D	REPETITION
6A	6B	6C	6D	ANTICIPATION

4B
STRUCTURE
OCCUPIED STRUCTURE

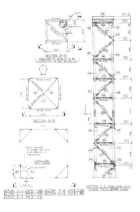

gradually increasing in biomass or structure.
the amounts of organic matter, acidity, and roots present that affect the aggregation of soil particles.
the study of the behavior of, and intersections among components in, a model of a complex system.
an operation in which the parts or elements of an object are transformed into new forms when combined.

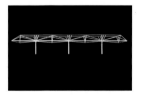

4C
STRUCTURE
SPACE / FRAME

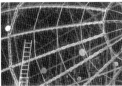

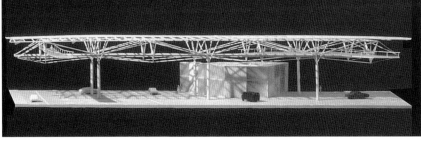

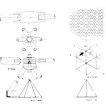

a patch attached to a corridor, both of the same landscape element type.
an intersection of corridors, and a source or sink of flows
of objects

FULLER WORLD EXPOSITION

4D
STRUCTURE
ROOF TYPOLOGIES

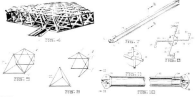

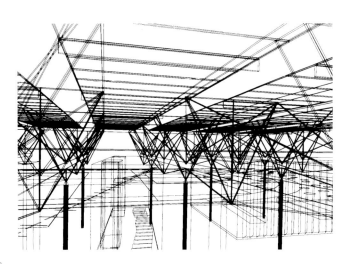

Plate 74
1. Model on the dock. Fig. 4. A perspective view of a representation
truss section of the roof and wall framework. Fig. 5. One of the
octahedrons and conjoined tetrahedrons of the truss. Fig. 6. Separated
views of the octahedra and tetrahedra units. Fig. 7. A perspective

view of one of the struts in Fig. 4. Fig. 8. A cross-section of the
strut in Fig. 7. Fig. 10. A side view of a modified strut. Fig. 11.
An end view of the strut in Fig. 10.

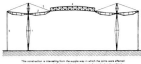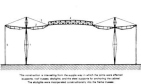

This construction is interesting from the supple way in which the joints were effected
in supports, roof trusses, skylights, and the steel supports for anchoring the cables.
The skylights were incorporated constructionally into the frame trusses.
the facade of aluminium and glass was hung curtainwise on the overhanging trusses.

a threshold of force below which a system returns
to its original state and above which it is somewhat
deformed.
a sequence of sets composed of smaller subsets.
methods that concurrently analyze many
factors, plus the relationships among the factors.
a measure of stability, referring to the time period
during which a certain characteristic continues to be present
at a given level.

1A	1B	1C	1D		SURFACE
2A	2B	2C	2D		SERVICE
3A	3B	3C	3D		ORGANIZATION
4A	4B	4C	4D		STRUCTURE
5A	5B	5C	5D		REPETITION
6A	6B	6C	6D		ANTICIPATION

5A
REPETITION
DETAIL DESIGN ELEMENTS

a study beginning with the individual attributes and building up to the broadest groupings of them.

a study of types, or a pre-classification

TIME:
Notations include time as a variable. It is not an accident that notations figure most significantly in that arts that unfold in time:music, dance, theater. If we allow, along with Paul Virilio, that the life of the city and its experience belongs more today to time than to space ("Now speed--ubiquity, instantaneousness -- dissolves the city, or rather displaces it, in time"), the special capacity of notation to make the thematic the measurement and unfolding of time takes on a special importance: interval, duration, tempo, acceleration, repetition and accumulation are key variables in the notational schema.

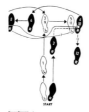

Dance Diagram, 1962
Synthetic polymer paint on canvas. 71 3/4 x 52 in. (182 x 132.1 cm)
Founding Collection Contribution
The Andy Warhol Foundation for the Visual Arts. Inc.

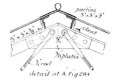

5. Infrastructures allow detailed design of typical elements or repetitive structures, facilitating an architectural approach to urbanism. Instead of moving always down in scale from the general to the specific, infrastructural design begins with the precise delineation of specific systems within specific limits. Unlike other models, (planning codes or typological norms for example), that tend to schematize and regulate architectural form, and work by prohibition, the limits to architectural design in infrastructural complexes are technical and instrumental. In infrastructural urbanism, form matters, but more for what it can do than for what it looks like.

1A	1B	1C	1D		SURFACE
2A	2B	2C	2D		SERVICE
3A	3B	3C	3D		ORGANIZATION
4A	4B	4C	4D		STRUCTURE
5A	5B	5C	5D		REPETITION
6A	6B	6C	6D		ANTICIPATION

5B
REPETITION
PATCH TYPOLOGIES 1

1. The variables in organizational diagrams include formal and programmatic configurations: space and event, force and resistance, density, distribution and direction. Organization always implies both program and its distribution in space, bypassing conventional dichotomies of function vs. form or form vs. content. A diagram is not a thing in itself, but rather a description of potential relationships among elements.

DIDEROT: MILITARY FORMULATIONS

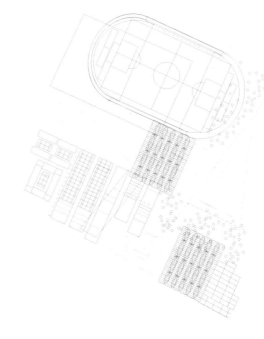

PLAN PATCH

REPETITION
PATCH TYPOLOGIES 2

2. Unlike classical theories based on imitation, diagrams do not map or represent already existing objects or systems but anticipate new organizations and specify yet to be realized relationships. They are not simply a reduction from an existing order; their abstraction is instrumental, not an end in itself. Simplified and highly graphic, they can be loosely interpreted. They work as "abstract machines" and do not resemble what they produce.

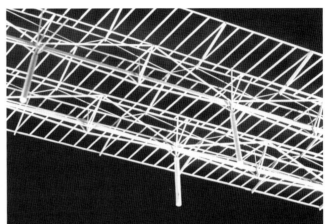

the integration of structure and function, i.e., the spatial configuration and the patterns of flows in a landscape.
a regime, subject to minor environmental changes, that fluctuates but remains in equilibrium.
the distribution of energy, materials, and species in relation to the sizes, shapes, numbers, kinds and configurations of landscape elements or ecosystems.

WAVE FORMATIONS

REPETITION
FIELDS—VARIATION / REPETITION

3. Diagrams are not "decoded" according to universal conventions; rather, the relationships are transposed – moved part by part into a new organizational context: "Whereas translation excludes all particulars in favor of a general equivalent, the transposition of media is accomplished serially, at discrete points. [....] Because the number of elements and the rules of association are hardly ever identical, every transposition is to a degree arbitrary, a manipulation. It can appeal to nothing universal and must therefore leave gaps."

—FRIEDRICH A. KITTLER

the pattern of spatial arrangement of individuals, such as regular, random, or clustered.
a significantly nonrandom spatial pattern
the degree to which one or a few species predominate in a community in terms of numbers, biomass, or dynamics.

Figure 8. Progression of clear-cutting on a grid pattern using the dispersed-patch model, in which areas are selected for cutting so as to be regularly distributed through the landscape. Shading indicates the (A) 25 percent, (B) 50 percent, and (C) 75 percent cutover points.

6A
ANTICIPATION
EVENT SCAFFOLD

the maximum number of individuals or maximum biomass that a particular environment can support
a threshold at which the continuity in structure and
function of a system is easily altered or broken

Figure 10.6 Movement of a striped skunk during a single winter night, as determined from tracks in snow. Solid lines are hedgerows, single dashed lines indicate borders of crops within a field, double solid lines indicate a road, and double dashed lines indicate a narrow dirt road. (From B. J. Verts, The Biology of the Striped Skunk, copyright 1967 by the Board of Trustees of the University of Illinois.)

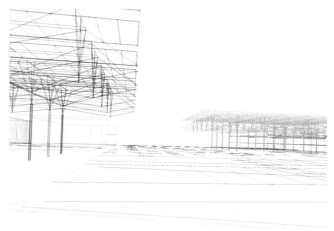

6. Infrastructures are flexible and anticipatory. They work with time and are open to change. By specifying what must be fixed and what is subject to change, they can be precise and indeterminate at the same time. they work through man-agement and cultivation, changing slowly to adjust to shifting conditions. They do not progress toward a predetermined state (as with master planning strategies), but are always evolving within a loose envelope of constraints.

88

6B
ANTICIPATION
PASSIVE PROGRAMS

ANTICIPATION:
Notations describe a work that is yet to be realized. Even if already performed, the work described is open to interpretation and change in the course of future per-formance. In this sense, notation is optimistic and anticipatory. Unlike classical theories of mimeses, nota-tions do not map or represent already exisitng objects or systems but anticipate new organizations and spec-ify yet to be realized relationships. Notation is not about interrogation, critique or commentary. These "critical" practices utilize notation's discursive capaci-ties only in retrospect, (pointing out what is wrong with existing reality) whereas notation's more radical possi-bility lies in the possibility of proposing alternative real-ities. Notation's special properties can be expoited by the urban designer' to produce a kind of "directed inde-terminancy:" proposals that are robust and specific enough to sustain change over time, yet open enough to support multiple interpretations.

a directional species replacement process, often lead-ing though a series of recognizable stages to a climax com-munity.
the smallest homogenous unit visible at the spatial scale of landscape.
an event or characteristic; e.g., in evolution or geologic history, that causes or controls a proximate factor.
a spot that is colonized by a species, that is, when the species arrives and successfully reproduces and grows.

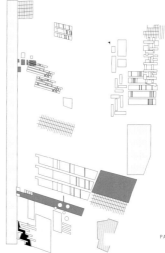

PASSIVE PROGRAMS

6C
ANTICIPATION
ACTIVE

PERFORMANCE:

This project marks a shift away from issues of representation, to engage architecture as a material practice. Material practices, (ecology, or engineering for example) do not work primarily with images or meaning but with performance: energy inputs and outputs, the calibration of force and resistance. They are less concerned with what things look like and more concerned with what they can do. Material practices do not attempt to control or predetermine meaning. Instead, they go beyond the paradoxes of the linguistic to examine the effects of signifying practices on performance and behavior. Although these material practices work instrumentally, they are not limited to the direct manipulation of given material. Instead they project transformations of reality by means of abstract techniques such as notation, simulation or calculation.

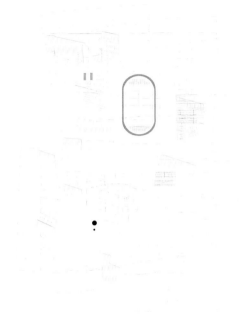

a measure of stability, referring to the time period during which a certain characteristic continues to be present at a given level.

the condition in which a landscape subjected to severe disturbance does not return fully to its previous equilibrium level.

survival of species with irregular fluctuations because of disturbance or unpredictable (stochastic) events.

a process of increasing efficiency or planning for increased efficiency, usually one among several characteristics.

ACTIVE PROGRAMS

6D
ANTICIPATION
PROGRAM SCORES

COLLECTIVE:

Notations presume a social context, and shared conventions of interpretation. The score is not a work itself, but a set of instructions for performing a work. A score cannot be a private language. It works instrumentally to coordinate the actions of multiple performers who collectively produce the work as event. As a model for operating in the city, the collective character of notation is highly suggestive. Going beyond transgression and cross-programming, notations could function to map the complex and indeterminate theater of everyday life in the city. The use of notation might provoke a shift from the production of space to the performance of space.

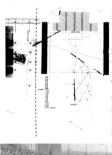

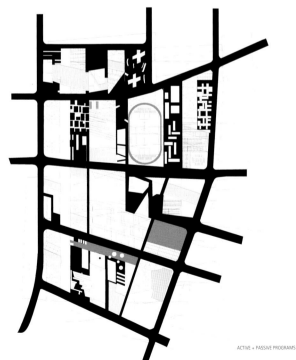

a process of forming a number of cities surrounded by suburbia.

the particular species present, for example in a community.

changes in a community due to colonization, extinction, and population size fluctuation.

an area (usually large) from which species come in colonization.

ACTIVE + PASSIVE PROGRAMS

Field

"The order is not rationalistic and underlying but is simply order,

Conditions

like that of continuity, one thing after another."   DONALD JUDD

PROJECTS

Korean-American Museum of Art, Los Angeles, 1995

National Diet Library, Kansai Kan, Japan, 1996

Amy Lipton Gallery, New York, 1989–91. Detail

The field describes a space of propagation, of effects. It contains *no matter or material points*, rather functions, vectors and speeds. It describes local relations of difference within fields of celerity, transmission or of careering points, in a word, what Minkowski called the *world*." SANFORD KWINTER, 1986[1]

01 FROM OBJECT TO FIELD

Field conditions moves from the one toward the many, from individuals to collectives, from objects to fields. In its most complex manifestation, the concept of field conditions refers to mathematical field theory, to nonlinear dynamics, and to computer simulations of evolutionary change. However, my understanding of field conditions in architecture is somewhat distinct from its more exact meaning in the physical sciences. I intend the phrase to resonate with a more tactical sense, as it would for an anthropologist or a botanist engaged in "fieldwork," for a general facing the field of battle, or the architect who cautions a builder to "verify in field." My concern parallels a shift in recent technologies from the analog to the digital. It pays close attention to precedents in visual art, from the abstract painting of Piet Mondrian in the 1920s to minimalist and postminimalist sculpture of the 1960s. Postwar composers, as they moved away from the strictures of serialism, employed concepts such as "clouds" of sound or, in the case of Iannis Xenakis, "statistical" music in which complex acoustical events cannot be broken down into their constituent elements.[2] The infra-structural elements of the modern city, by their nature linked together in open-ended networks, offer another example of field conditions in the urban context. A complete examination of the implications of field conditions in architecture would necessarily reflect the complex and dynamic behaviors of architecture's users, and speculate on new methodologies to model program and space.

To generalize, a field condition could be any formal or spatial matrix capable of unifying diverse elements while respecting the identity of each. Field configurations are loosely bound aggregates characterized by porosity and local interconnectivity. Overall shape and extent are highly fluid and less important than the internal relationships of parts, which determine the behavior of the field. Field conditions are bottom-up phenomena, defined not by overarching geometrical schemas but by intricate local connections. Interval, repetition, and seriality are key concepts. Form matters, but not so much the forms of things as the forms *between* things.

Field conditions cannot claim to produce a systematic theory of architectural form or composition. The theoretical model proposed here anticipates its own irrelevance when faced with the realities of practice. These are working concepts derived from experimentation in contact with the real.

0.2 GEOMETRIC VS. ALGEBRAIC COMBINATION

The diverse elements of classical architecture are organized into coherent wholes by means of geometric systems of proportion.

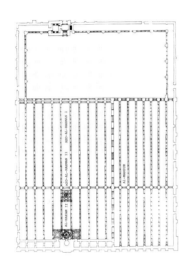

The Great Mosque of
Cordoba, Spain, c. 785–800.
Shaded area indicates
original extent

The Great Mosque of Cordoba, Spain, constructed over a span of nearly eight centuries, offers an instructive counterexample.[3] The form of the mosque had been clearly established: an enclosed forecourt, flanked by a minaret tower, opening onto a covered space for worship (perhaps derived from market structures, or adapted from the Roman basilica). The enclosure is loosely oriented toward the *qibla*, a continuous prayer wall marked by a small niche (the *mihrab*). In the first stage of construction (c. 785–800) the typological precedent was respected, resulting in a simple structure of ten parallel walls perpendicular to the *qibla*. These walls, supported on columns and pierced by arches, defining a covered space of equal dimension to the open court. The arched walls operate in counterpoint to the framed vistas across the grain of the space. The columns are located at the intersection of these two vectors, forming an undifferentiated but highly charged field. This field generates complex parallax effects that prey on visitors as they move through the space. The entire west wall is open to the courtyard, so that once within the precinct of the mosque there is no single entrance. The axial, processional space of the Christian church gives way to a nondirectional space, a serial order of "one thing after another."[4]

The mosque was subsequently enlarged in four stages. Significantly, with each addition the fabric of the original has remained substantially intact. The typological structure is reiterated at larger scale, while the local relationships have remained fixed. By comparison with classical Western architecture, it is possible to identify

Although ratios can be expressed numerically, the relationships intended are fundamentally geometric. Alberti's well know axiom that "Beauty is the consonance of the parts such that nothing can be added or taken away" expresses an ideal of organic geometric unity. The conventions of classical architecture dictate not only the proportions of individual elements but also the relationship between individual elements. Parts form ensembles which in turn form larger wholes. Precise rules of axiality, symmetry, or formal sequence govern the organization of the whole. Classical architecture displays a wide variation on these rules, but the principle of hierarchical distribution of parts to whole is constant. Individual elements are maintained in hierarchical order by extensive geometric relationships in order to preserve overall unity.

contrasting principles of combination: one *algebraic*, working with numerical units combined one after another, and the other *geometric*, working with figures (lines, planes, solids) organized in space to form larger wholes.[5] In Cordoba, for example, independent elements are combined additively to form an indeterminate whole. The relations of part to part are identical in the first and last versions constructed. The local syntax is fixed, but there is no overarching geometric scaffolding. Parts are not fragments of wholes, but simply parts. Unlike the idea of closed unity enforced in western classical architecture, the structure can be added onto without substantial morphological transformation. Field configurations are inherently expandable; the possibility of incremental growth is anticipated in the mathematical relations of the parts.

It could be argued that there are numerous examples of classical Western buildings that have grown incrementally and have been transformed over time. St. Peter's in Rome, for example has an equally long history of construction and rebuilding. But there is a significant difference. At St. Peter's, additions are morphological transformations, elaborating and extending a basic geometric schema, and tending toward compositional closure. This contrasts with the mosque at Cordoba where each stage replicates and preserves the previous stage of construction by the addition of similar parts. And at Cordoba, even in later stages when the mosque was consecrated as Christian church and a Gothic cathedral was inserted into the continuous and undifferentiated fabric of the mosque, the existing spatial order resisted the central or axial focus

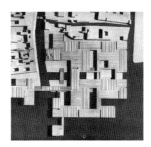

Le Corbusier, Venice Hospital, 1964–65

typical of the Western church. As Rafael Moneo has observed: "I do not believe that the Cordoba Mosque has been destroyed by all these modifications. Rather, I think that the fact that the mosque continues to be itself in face of all these interventions is a tribute to its own integrity."[6]

To briefly extend the argument to a more recent example, Le Corbusier's Venice Hospital (1964–65) employs a syntax of repeated self-same parts, establishing multiple links at its periphery with the city fabric. The project develops horizontally, through a logic of accumulation. The basic block of program, the "care unit" formed of twenty-eight beds, is repeated throughout. Consulting rooms occupy open circulation spaces in the covered areas between. The rotating placement of blocks establishes connections and pathways from ward to ward, while the displacement of the blocks opens up voids within the horizontal field of the hospital. There is no single focus, no unifying geometric schema. As in the mosque at Cordoba, the overall form is an elaboration of conditions established locally.[7]

0.3 WALKING OUT OF CUBISM

Barnett Newman, it has been said, used a sequence of plane/line/plane to "walk out of the imperatives of cubist space and close the door behind him."[8] The story of postwar American painting and sculpture is in large part a story of this effort to move beyond the limits of cubist compositional syntax. Sculptors in particular, working under the shadow of the achievements of abstract expressionist painting, felt that a complex language of faceted planes and figural fragments inherited from prewar European artists was inadequate to their larger ambitions. It is out of this sense of exhaustion that minimalism emerged in the mid-sixties. Robert Morris's refusal of composition in favor of process, or Donald Judd's critique of "composition by parts" evidence this effort to produce a new model for working that might be as simple and immediate as the painting of the previous decades they so admired.

Minimalist work of the sixties and seventies sought to empty the artwork of its figurative or decorative character in order to foreground its architectural condition. The construction of meaning was displaced from the object itself to the spatial field between the viewer and the object: a fluid zone of perceptual interference, populated by moving bodies. Artists such as Carl Andre, Dan Flavin, Morris, and Judd sought to go beyond formal or compositional variation to engage the space of the gallery and the body of the viewer. In written statements, both Judd and Morris express their skepticism toward European (i.e., cubist) compositional norms. They place their work instead in the context of recent American developments.

Donald Judd, installation view, Marfa, Texas

As Morris wrote: "European art since Cubism has been a history of permuting relationships around the general premise that relationships should remain critical. American art has developed by uncovering successive premises for making itself."[9] Both Morris and Judd single out Jackson Pollock for his decisive contribution. Judd notes that "Most sculpture is made part by part, by addition, composed." For Judd, what is required is consolidation: "In the new work the shape, image, color and surface are single and not partial and scattered. There aren't any neutral or moderate areas or parts, any connections or transitional areas."[10] The aspirations of minimalist work are therefore toward unitary forms, direct use of industrial materials, and simple combinations: a "pre-executive" clarity of intellectual and material terms. Minimalism's decisive tectonic shift activated the viewing space and reasserted the artwork's condition as "specific object."

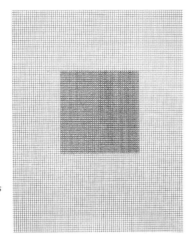

96

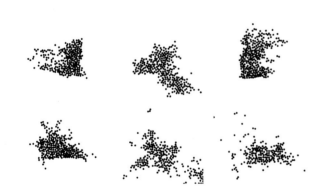

And yet if minimalism represents a significant overturning of prewar compositional principles, it remains indebted to certain essentializing models in its reductive formal language and use of materials. Its objects are clearly delimited and solidly constructed. (Judd's later architectural constructions confirm this essential tectonic conservatism.) Minimalism develops in sequences, but rarely in fields. It is for this reason that the work of artists usually designated "postminimal" is of particular interest here.[11] In contrast to Andre or Judd, the work of artists such as Bruce Nauman, Lynda Benglis, Keith Sonnier, Alan Saret, Eva Hesse, and Barry Le Va is materially diverse and improper. Words, movement, technology, fluid and perishable materials, representations of the body—all of these "extrinsic" contents that minimalism had repressed—return. Postminimalism is marked by hesitation and ontological doubt where the minimalists are definitive; it is painterly and informal where the minimalists are restrained; it remains committed to tangible things and visibility where the minimalists are concerned with underlying structures and ideas. These works, from the wire constructions of Alan Saret to the pourings of Lynda Benglis to the "nonsites" of Robert Smithson, introduce chance and contingency into the work of art. They shift even more radically the perception of the work, from discrete object to a record of the process of its making in the field.

The artist who moves most decisively in the direction of what I am calling field conditions is Barry Le Va. Partly trained as an architect, Le Va is acutely aware of the spatial field implicated by

Barry Le Va, *Six Blown Lines*, 1969

the material. Instead the artist establishes the conditions within which the material will be deployed, and then directs its flows. In the case of Le Va's pieces of felt cloth, it is a matter of relating fold to fold, line to line. In later works from the sixties, the materials themselves become so ephemeral as to function as a delicate registration of process and change.

0.4 THICK 2D: MOIRÉS, MATS

the sculptural work. Beginning in the mid-sixties, he began making pieces, some planned in advance, others incorporating random process, that thoroughly dissolve the idea of "sculpture" as a delimited entity, an object distinct from the field it occupies. He called these works "distributions": "Whether 'random' or 'orderly' a 'distribution' is defined as 'relationships of points and configurations to each other' or concomitantly, 'sequences of events.'"[12] Local relationships are more important than overall form. The generation of form through "sequences of events" is somewhat related to the generative rules for flock behavior or algebraic combination. Le Va signals a key compositional principle emerging out of postminimalism: the displacement of control to a series of intricate local rules for combination, or as a "sequences of events," but not as an overall formal configuration. In the case of postminimalism, this is often related to material choices. When working with materials such as wire mesh (Saret), poured latex (Benglis), or blown flour (Le Va), the artist simply cannot exercise a precise formal control over

All grids are fields, but not all fields are grids. One of the potentials of the field is to redefine the relation between figure and ground. If we think of the figure not as a demarcated object read against a stable field, but as an effect emerging from the field itself—as moments of intensity, as peaks or valleys within a continuous field—than it might be possible to imagine figure and field as more closely allied. What is intended here is a close attention to the production of difference at the local scale, even while maintaining a relative indifference to the form of the whole. Authentic and productive social differences, it is suggested, thrive at the local level, and not in the form of large scale semiotic messages or sculptural forms. Hence the study of these field combinations would be a study of models that work in the zone between figure and abstraction, models that refigure the conventional opposition between figure and abstraction, or systems of organization capable of producing vortexes, peaks, and protuberances out of individual elements that are themselves regular or repetitive.

Field conditions diagrams

A moiré is a figural effect produced by the superposition of two regular fields. Unexpected effects, exhibiting complex and apparently irregular behaviors result from the combination of elements that are in and of themselves repetitive and regular. But moiré effects are not random. They shift abruptly in scale, and repeat according to complex mathematical rules. Moiré effects are often used to measure hidden stresses in continuous fields, or to map complex figural forms. In either case there is an uncanny coexistence of a regular field and emergent figure.

In the architectural or urban context, the example of moiré effects begs the question of the surface. The field *is* fundamentally a horizontal phenomenon—even a graphic one—and all of the examples described thus far function in the plan dimension. Although certain postmodern cities (Tokyo for example) might be characterized as fully three dimensional fields, the prototypical cities of the late twentieth century are distinguished by horizontal extension. What these field combinations seem to promise in this context is a thickening and intensification of experience at specified moments within the extended field of the city. The monuments of the past, including the skyscraper, a modernist monument to efficient production, stood out from the fabric of the city as privileged vertical moments. The new institutions of the city will perhaps occur at moments of intensity, linked to the wider network of the urban field, and marked by not by demarcating lines but by thickened surfaces.

98

LEFT: Moiré pattern

BELOW: Diagram of moiré grates

BOTTOM: Reindeer herd reacting to helicopter overhead

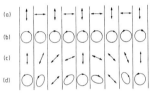

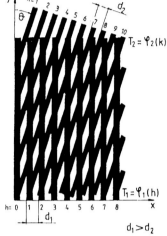

0.5 FLOCKS, SCHOOLS, SWARMS, CROWDS

In the late 1980s, artificial intelligence theorist Craig Reynolds created a computer program to simulate the flocking behavior of birds. As described by M. Mitchel Waldrop in *Complexity: The Emerging Science at the Edge of Order and Chaos*, Reynolds placed a large number of autonomous, birdlike agents, which he called "boids," into an on-screen environment. The boids were programmed to follow three simple rules of behavior: first, to maintain a minimum distance from other objects in the environment (obstacles as well as other boids); second, to match velocities with other boids in the neighborhood; third, to move toward the perceived center of mass of boids in its neighborhood. As Waldrop notes: "What is striking about these rules is that none of them said "Form a flock"…the rules were entirely local, referring only to what an individual boid could do and see in its own vicinity. If a flock was going to form at all, it would have to do so from the bottom up, as an emergent phenomenon. And yet flocks *did* form, every time."[13]

99

The flock is clearly a field phenomenon, defined by precise and simple local conditions, and relatively indifferent to overall form and extent. Because the rules are defined locally, obstructions are not catastrophic to the whole. Variations and obstacles in the environment are accommodated by fluid adjustment. A small flock and a large flock display fundamentally the same structure. Over many iterations, patterns emerge. Without repeating exactly, flock behavior tends toward roughly similar configurations, not as a fixed type, but as the cumulative result of localized behavior patterns.

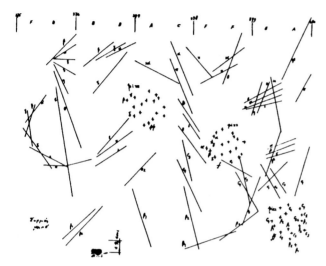

Iannis Xenakis, Syrmos, 1959. Graphic version of "fixed states" before transcription

Crowds present a different dynamic, motivated by more complex desires, and interacting in less predictable patterns. Elias Canetti in *Crowds and Power* has proposed a broader taxonomy: *open* and *closed* crowds; *rhythmic* and *stagnating* crowds; the *slow* crowd and the *quick* crowd. He examines the varieties of the crowd, from the religious throng formed by pilgrims to the mass of participants in spectacle, even extending his thoughts to the flowing of rivers, the piling up of crops, and the density of the forest. According to Canetti, the crowd has four primary attributes: "The crowd always wants to grow; Within a crowd there is equality; The crowd loves density; The crowd needs a direction."[14] The relation to Reynolds' rules outlined above is oblique, but visible. Canetti, however, is not interested in prediction or verification. His sources are literary, historical, and personal. Moreover, he is always aware that the crowd can be liberating as well as confining, angry and destructive as well as joyous.

Composer Iannis Xenakis conceived his early work *Metastasis* as the acoustical equivalent to the phenomenon of the crowd. Specifically, he was looking for a compositional technique adequate to express powerful personal memories:

Athens—an anti-Nazi demonstration—hundreds of thousands of people chanting a slogan which reproduces itself like a gigantic rhythm. Then combat with the enemy. The rhythm bursts into an enormous chaos of sharp sounds; the whistling of bullets; the crackling of machine guns. The sounds begin to disperse. Slowly silence falls back on the town. Taken uniquely from an aural point of view and detached from any other aspect these sound events made out of a large number of individual sounds are not separately perceptible, but reunite them again and a new sound is formed which may be perceived in its entirety. It is the same case with the song of the cicadas or the sound of hail or rain, the crashing of waves on the cliffs, the hiss of waves on the shingle.[15]

In attempting to reproduce these "global acoustical events," Xenakis drew upon his own considerable graphic imagination, and his training in descriptive geometry to invert conventional procedures of composition. That is to say, he began with a graphic notation describing the desired effect of "fields" or "clouds" of sound, and only later reduced these graphics to conventional musical notation. Working as he was with material that was beyond the order of magnitude of the available compositional techniques, he had to invent new procedures in order to choreograph the "characteristic distribution of vast numbers of events."[16]

Crowds and swarms operate at the edge of control. Aside from the suggestive formal possibilities, with these two examples architecture could profitably shift its attention from its traditional top-down forms of control and begin to investigate the possibilities of a more fluid, bottom-up approach. Field conditions offers a tentative opening in architecture to address the dynamics of use, behavior of crowds, and the complex geometries of masses in motion.

0.6 DISTRIBUTED INSTITUTIONS

There exists a strong historical connection between the precise rules of axiality, symmetry, and formal hierarchy that govern classical architecture and the traditional type-forms of Western institutions. The library, the museum, and the concert hall, as much as the bank, the city hall, or the capitol all appeal to the stability of classical order to signify their status as durable institutions. In the twentieth century, the utopian programs of early modern architecture sought to render the institutions of liberal democracy as transparent bodies. Lightweight steel skeletons and glass curtain walls signaled literal transparency, while a functional and compositional dynamic made visible the separate elements of these increasingly complex programs.

However, the extent to which compositional shifts are capable of refiguring these institutions reaches a limit. On the one hand, it should be noted that while the rules of combination may be new in these modernist compositions of fragments, the classical assumption that composition is concerned with the arrangement of and connections among those parts persists. As Robert Morris has put it, "European art since Cubism has been a history of permuting relationships around the general premise that *relationships should remain critical.*"[17] Perhaps a more radical shift is required. This is all the more urgent given that, under the pressure of technological or societal shifts, institutions are changing from within. As the social, political, and technical roles of those institutions are called into question, the corresponding typologies lose their special capacity to order and represent the space of these institutions. In the case of the library or the museum, what was once a place of certainty, an orderly deposit of knowledge arranged in familiar and agreed-upon categories, has been eroded by the onrush of media, consumer culture, and telecommunications. Architecture's capacity to represent and shelter that collective memory has in turn withered. To design a library or a museum today is to contend with an entirely new set of expectations. Above all, it means to recognize an ever increasing uncertainty about what constitutes knowledge, who has access to it and how it is distributed.

There are no simple equations of organization and behavior, of politics and form. As Michel Foucault has pointed out, while there are constraining architectures, there are no specifically "liberating" architectures. "Liberty," he says, "is a practice."[18] Nonhierarchical compositions cannot guarantee an open society or equality in politics. Democracy, it has been said, has less to do with the ability to do things as with the ability to undo things. The goal, therefore, in the final two projects presented in this volume is to rethink conventional institutional form through the concept of the field. The organizational principles proposed here suggest new definitions of "parts," and alternative ways of conceiving the question of relationships among those parts. The form of these institutions does not attempt to represent, metaphorically, the new condition of the institution, nor does it attempt to directly instigate new ways of thinking or behaving. Instead, by forming the institution within a directed field condition, connected to the city or the landscape, a space is left for the tactical improvisations of future users. A "loose fit" is proposed between activity and enclosing envelope.

Michel Serres's reminder that static, accidents, and disruptions will inevitably undermine any formal system defined by points and lines is not so far from what is intended here. More than a formal configuration, the field condition implies an architecture that admits change, accident, and improvisation. It is an architecture not invested in durability, stability, and certainty, but an architecture that leaves space for the uncertainty of the real:

> Stations and paths together form a system. Points and lines, beings and relations. What is interesting might be the construction of the system, the number and disposition of stations and paths. Or it might be the flow of messages passing through the lines. In other words, a complex system can be formally described....One might have sought the formation and distribution of the lines, paths, and stations, their borders, edges and forms. But one must write as well of the interceptions, of the accidents in the flow along the way between stations...What passes may be a message but parasites (static) prevent it from being heard, and sometimes, from being sent.[19]

NOTES:

1. Sanford Kwinter, "La Città Nuova: Modernity and Continuity" in *Zone 1/2* (New York, 1986), 88–9, emphasis added.

2. Xenakis uses language and concepts very close to those suggested here. See Nouritza Matossian, *Xenakis* (London: Kahn and Averill, 1990), 59.

3. The following discussion was adapted from Rafael Moneo: "La Vida de los edifcios" *Arquitecture* 256, (Sept.–Oct. 1985): 27–36.

4. This phrase is taken from Donald Judd's discussion of the paintings of Frank Stella: "The order is not rationalistic and underlying but is simply order, like that of continuity, one thing after another." Donald Judd, "Specific Objects," in *Complete Writings: 1959–1975* (Halifax: Nova Scotia College of Art and Design, 1975), 184.

5. The term *algebra* derives from the Arabic *al-jebr* "the reunion of broken parts." *Geometry*, on the other hand, is a word of Greek origin.

6. Moneo, "La Vida," 35.

7. Both the mosque at Cordoba and Le Corbusier's Venice Hospital figure in Alison Smithson's 1974 article "How to Recognise and Read Mat-Building," *Architectural Design* XLIV, 9 (1974): 573–90.

8. Cited in Rosalind Krauss, "Richard Serra: Sculpture Redrawn," *Artforum* (May 1972).

9. Robert Morris, "Anti Form," *Artforum* (April 1968), 34.

10. Judd, "Specific Objects," 183.

11. In fact, postminimalism developed at nearly the same time as minimalism. "Post" here implies a certain degree of dependence and opposition rather than chronological sequence. Note, for example, the absence of women in the ranks of the minimalists; postminimalism would be unthinkable without the contributions of Lynda Benglis or Eva Hesse. A certain fluidity in these categories is also required; Robert Morris, for example, is often grouped with the postminimalists. See Robert Pincus-Witten, "Introduction to Postminimalism" (1977) in *Postminimalism to Maximalism: American Art, 1966–1986* (Ann Arbor, MI: UMI Research Press, 1987).

12. Jane Livingston, "Barry Le Va: Distributional Sculpture," *Artforum* (November 1968).

13. M. Mitchel Waldrop, *Complexity: The Emerging Science at the Edge of Order and Chaos* (New York: Simon and Schuster, 1992), 240–1.

14. Elias Canetti, *Crowds and Power* (New York: Farrar, Straus and Giroux, 1984), 29.

15. Matossian, *Xenakis,* cited from an interview, 58.

16. Ibid., 58–9.

17. Morris, "Anti Form," 34, my emphasis.

18. Michel Foucault, "Nietzsche, Genealogy, History" in *The Foucault Reader*, ed. Paul Rabinow (New York: Pantheon, 1984), 87.

19. Michel Serres, *The Parasite*, trans. Lawrence R. Schehr (Baltimore: Johns Hopkins University Press, 1982), 10–1.

Korean–American Museum of Art, Los Angeles

COMPETITION, 1995

ARCHITECT: Stan Allen

ASSISTED BY: Lyn Rice, Katherine Kim, Chris Perry

SITE MODEL: Michael Silver

0.1 LOOSE-FIT URBANISM

The building proposes an urbanism characteristic of Los Angeles: long and low, horizontally layered, filled in but not densely packed. Taking its place in a streetscape characterized above all by its lack of consistency, the external form of the Korean-American Museum of Art is indifferent to its immediate context. Instead, the organizational effort is directed inside, articulating relations of program and the play of solid and void within a generic volume. The property line of the site is taken as the limit of the building, forming a loosely protected precinct. Within this oversize envelope, the elements of the program rattle around, opening up indeterminate interstitial spaces. Galleries form punctual figures within a generic field, while collective functions (lobby, cafe, lecture hall, bookshop) occupy the space between. The building mixes the large and the small, resolving the conflicts of the site through multiple scales.

0.2 INFRASTRUCTURES

The lower level of the museum is treated as an exposed foundation that serves to raise the main body of the museum above the street. A complex series of paths establish multiple links between the museum and the neighborhood while ensuring the autonomy of the exhibition level. Additional public functions occupy the site at this level according to the rigorous logic of the parallel walls that divide the site.

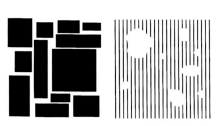

LEFT: **Patchwork diagram**

RIGHT: **Striated-field diagram**

OPPOSITE: **Context: Paramount Studios**

0.3 BLANK BOXES

The collection is housed in a number of discreet gallery volumes distributed throughout the main floor. These blank boxes maintain an appropriate degree of separation, control, and autonomy for the works of art displayed within, without dictating a rigid processional sequence. Curatorial intervention is necessarily concentrated and punctual. Tall skylights distribute diffused light to the galleries, giving them a character distinct from the public spaces, where transparent glazing opens horizontally to the city around.

0.4 COMPLEX CONTAINERS

The intention is to create an indeterminate space at the intersection of two known sets: the given perimeter of the site, and the gallery program. Instead of introducing complex geometries from outside, the project achieves complexity by articulating simple differences of scale and number. The project works by exploiting the incompatibility of container and contained. Its program is treated not as a single organism, but rather as an aggregate of smaller elements. This is an architecture that operates urbanistically, giving the effect of moving through a city street, introducing a temporal and programmatic complexity to the experience of the museum.

106

Model view

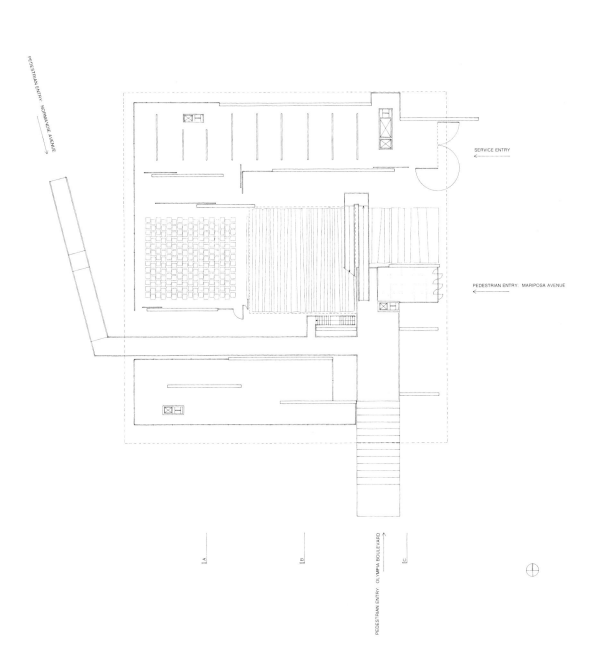

Ground-level plan

108

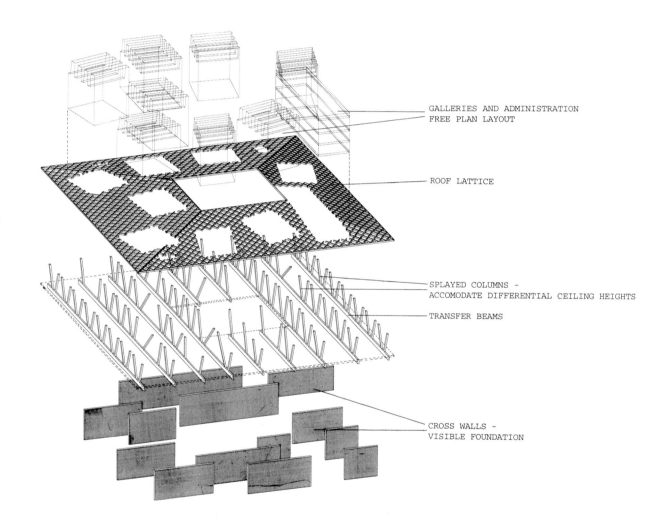

GALLERIES AND ADMINISTRATION
FREE PLAN LAYOUT

ROOF LATTICE

SPLAYED COLUMNS -
ACCOMODATE DIFFERENTIAL CEILING HEIGHTS

TRANSFER BEAMS

CROSS WALLS -
VISIBLE FOUNDATION

ABOVE: Diagram of structural systems

OPPOSITE: Montage of ground floor on site

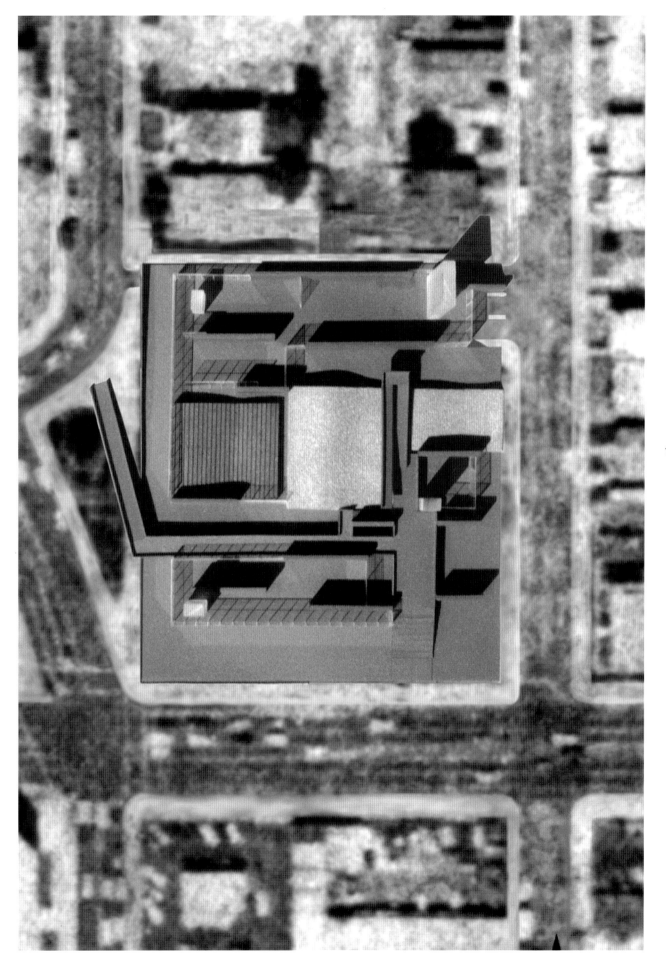

Model of gallery-level

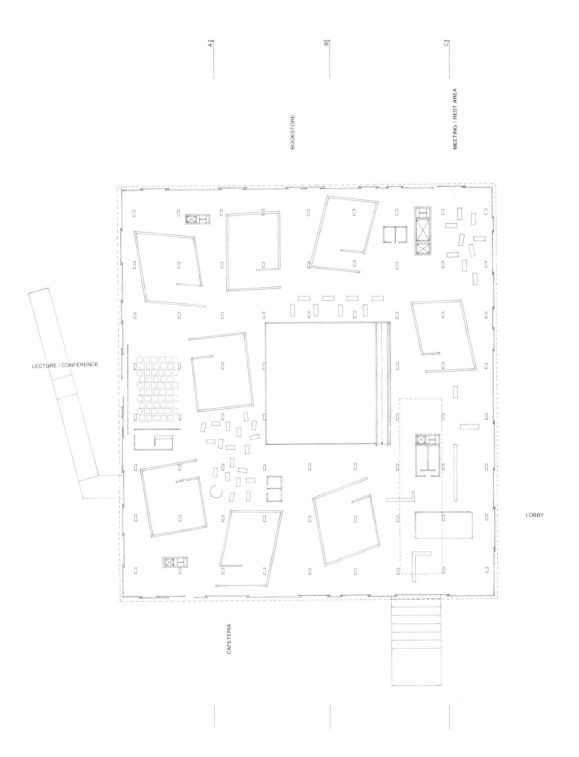

A

BOOKSTORE

B

C

MEETING / REST AREA

LECTURE / CONFERENCE

LOBBY

CAFETERIA

Gallery-level plan

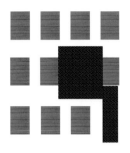

Undifferentiated program

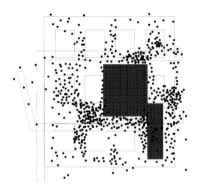

Activity clusters

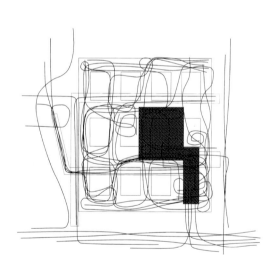

Movement patterns

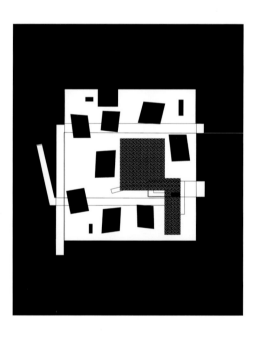

Figure/ground reversal

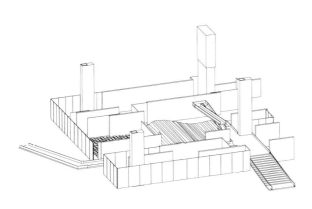

Enclosure and access

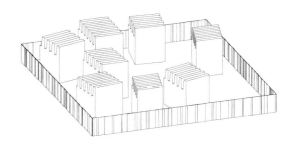

Gallery *recinto*

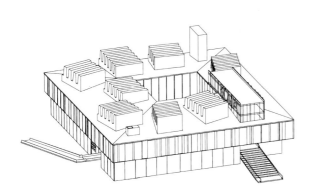

Massing

Gardens and paths

Elevation of site model

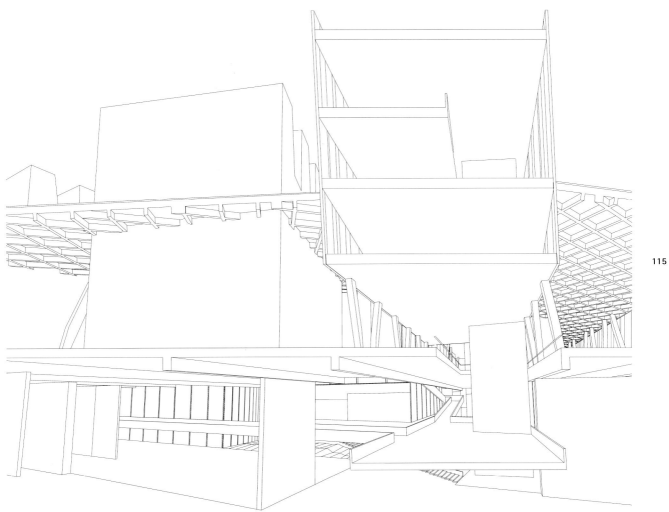

Sectional perspective

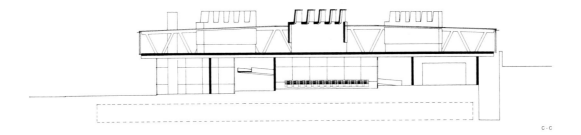

C - C

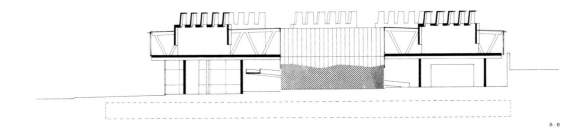

B - B

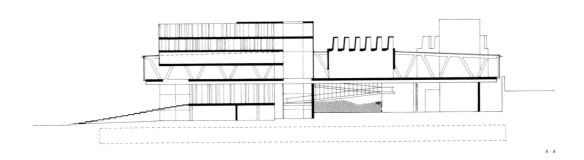

A - A

ABOVE: Cross-sections

OPPOSITE: Detail model

118

Street elevation

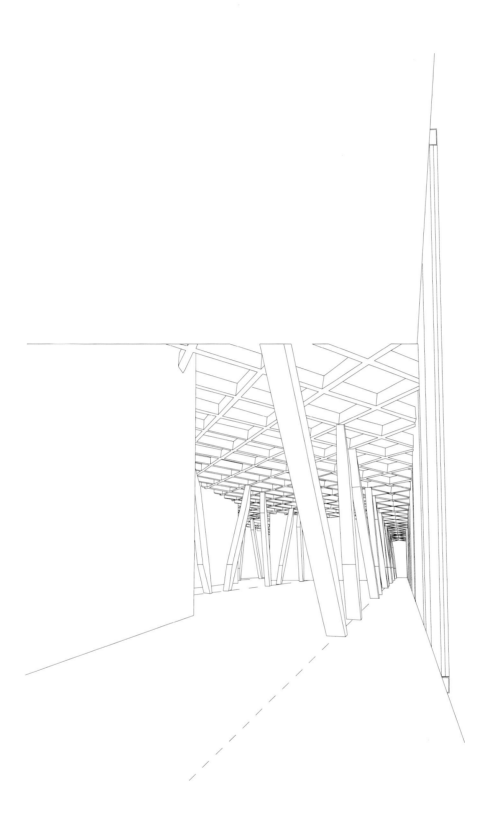

Gallery-level interior perspective

National Diet Library, Kansai Kan, Japan

COMPETITION PROJECT, 1996

ARCHITECT: Stan Allen

ASSISTED BY: Tsuto Sakamoto, Mieko Sakamoto,
and Troels Rugbjerg

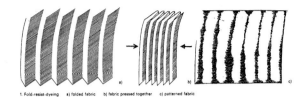

1. Fold-resist-dyeing   a) folded fabric   b) fabric pressed together   c) patterned fabric

ABOVE: Fabric dyeing process

OPPOSITE: Snead structural stack system

The given site for the National Diet Library in the Kansai Science City presents a condition of nonsite—an almost complete absence of local context. For this reason, we imposed a rhythm of landscaped areas—hard, soft, hard, soft—over the given band of buildable land, materializing an autonomous order on the surface of the site. In the absence of context, an artificial nature is proposed.

The public spaces are located at ground level in continuity with the manmade landscape. Instead of a traditional civic space separated from nature, the reading rooms and collective functions are seen as the extension of the landscape, a vast information garden where readers inhabit the paths, fields, courts, and clearings in a forest of columns. New technologies allow the distribution and exchange of information without the weighty apparatus of traditional institutions.

The function of the modern library is two-fold: the storage and protection of materials (archival) and the distribution of that material (informational). In a closed stack library, these two aspects are normally separated, resulting in a "black box" condition where the reader looses all contact with the archival material. We wanted the users of the library to constantly feel the presence of the vast quantity of material stored in the library. To that end, we have utilized a variant of the "Snead Stack System," a structural stack system common in the United States in the beginning of this century. By updating the structural technology of the Snead system, we can accommodate the circulating collection in a dense structural matrix occupying the very center of the building, visible to the readers and researchers within, and functioning as a symbolic marker from the outside.

Programs are distributed without hierarchy over the built area of the site. Connections between elements are governed by functional necessity and not by processional sequence. The envelope of the building is loosely drawn around this distributed order, forming a loose separation between the site and the events housed within.

121

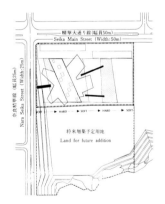

Site diagram

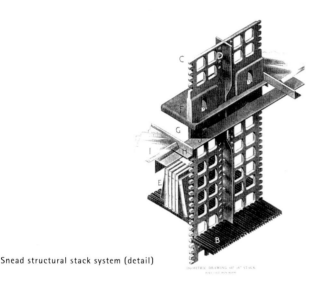

Snead structural stack system (detail)

INOMETRIC DRAWING OF 14" STACK

122

Partial transparencies reveal the mismatch of container and contained. These residual spaces between the envelope and the program elements within allow a programmatic indeterminacy where the function of the library can be extended or supplemented by new collective programs.

Reading rooms and primary public functions (entry, cafe, lockers, bookstore) are all located on the ground floor, in continuity with the landscaped site. Circulation stations are served by conveyors from the stacks above and compact storage below. Instead of being centralized in a single location, the functions of the "Information Exchange" have been distributed throughout the site as a series of information islands.

Administration, auditorium, research, and library exchange (semipublic functions) are housed in an interconnected network of bridges running at level 16.4 feet (5.5 meters) above the main public level. These functions are positioned to be visually continuous with the public spaces of the library yet in close proximity to the stacks.

Circulating stacks form a spine at the middle of the site, lifted above the public and administrative functions. Circulation stations are located at either end of the spine for efficient distribution of materials by conveyor to the reading rooms below. Compact stacks are located below grade.

Site access is from Seika Street, which opens onto a landscaped parking lot, located within the 131 foot (40 meter) setback line. Visitors move through landscaped gardens to the entry on the east façade of the building. Service access is from Nara Seika Street, opening directly into the basement service areas.

Footprint diagrams

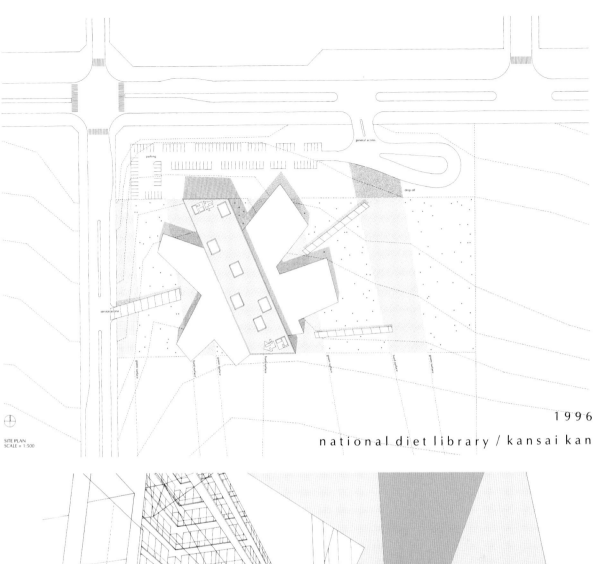

SITE PLAN
SCALE = 1:500

1996

national diet library / kansai kan

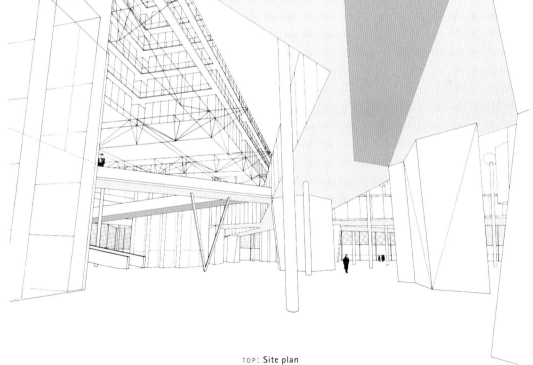

TOP: Site plan

BOTTOM: Interior perspective (reading room and stacks)

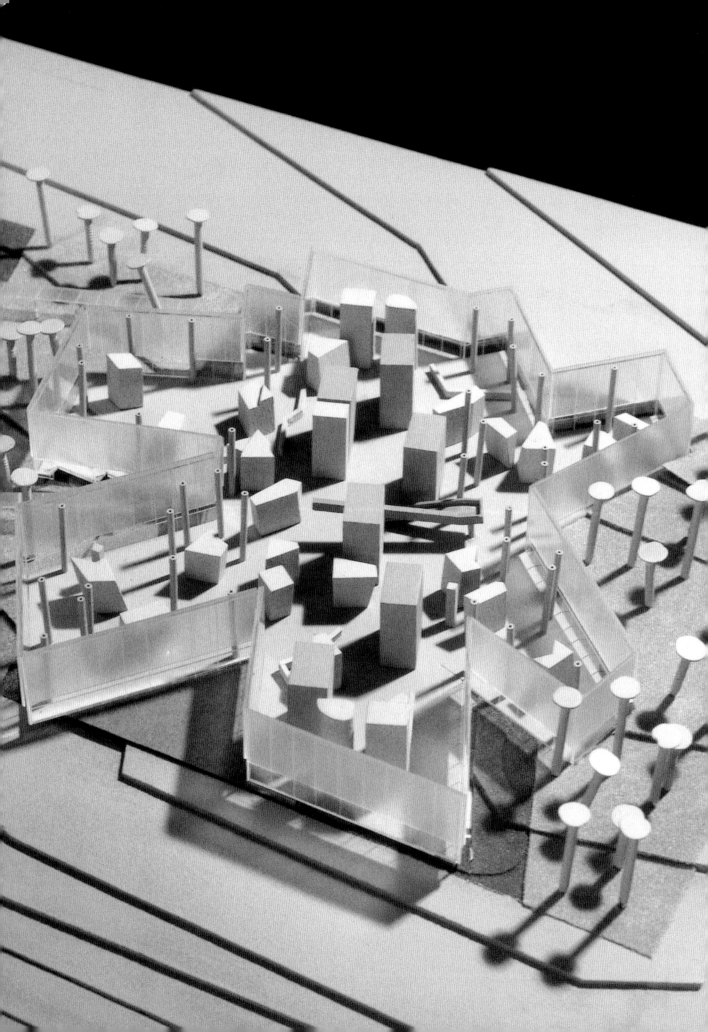

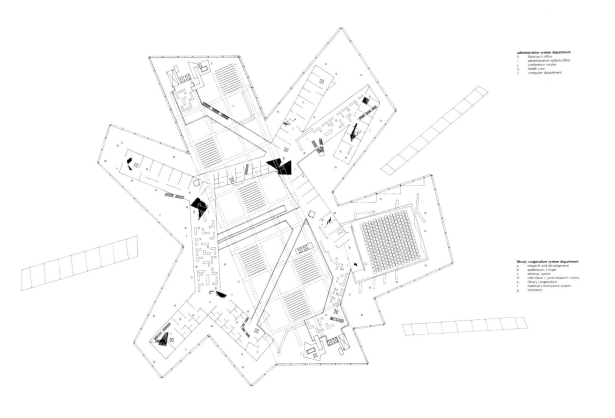

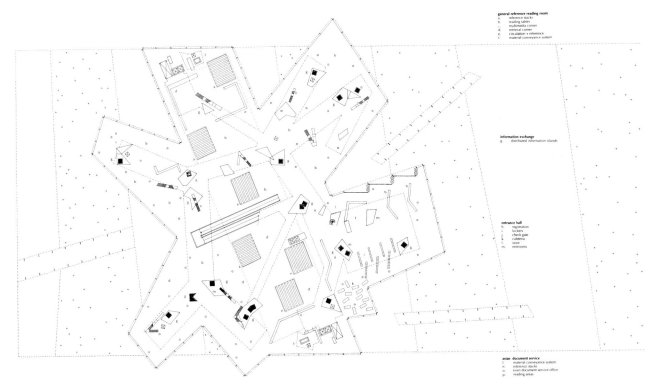

TOP: Ground-level plan

BOTTOM: Mezzanine-level plan

OPPOSITE: Site model (information landscape)

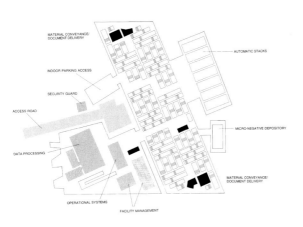

MATERIAL CONVEYANCE/
DOCUMENT DELIVERY

INDOOR PARKING ACCESS

SECURITY GUARD

ACCESS ROAD

DATA PROCESSING

OPERATIONAL SYSTEMS

FACILITY MANAGEMENT

AUTOMATIC STACKS

MICRO-NEGATIVE DEPOSITORY

MATERIAL CONVEYANCE/
DOCUMENT DELIVERY

Service level

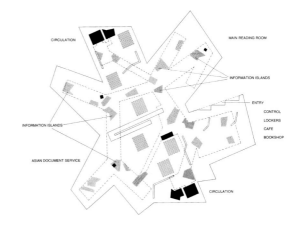

CIRCULATION

INFORMATION ISLANDS

ASIAN DOCUMENT SERVICE

MAIN READING ROOM

INFORMATION ISLANDS

ENTRY

CONTROL

LOCKERS

CAFE

BOOKSHOP

CIRCULATION

Entry level

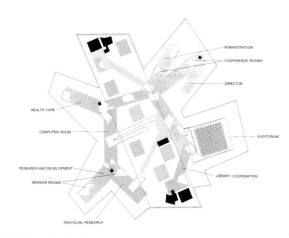

HEALTH CARE

COMPUTER ROOM

RESEARCH AND DEVELOPMENT

SEMINAR ROOMS

INDIVIDUAL RESEARCH

ADMINISTRATION

CONFERENCE ROOMS

DIRECTOR

AUDITORIUM

LIBRARY COOPERATION

Administration level

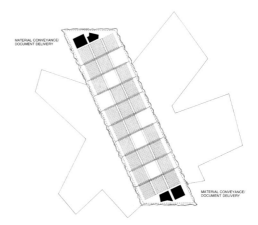

MATERIAL CONVEYANCE/
DOCUMENT DELIVERY

MATERIAL CONVEYANCE/
DOCUMENT DELIVERY

Stack level

Plan diagrams

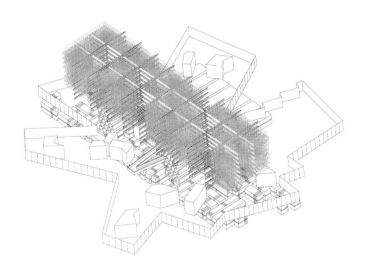

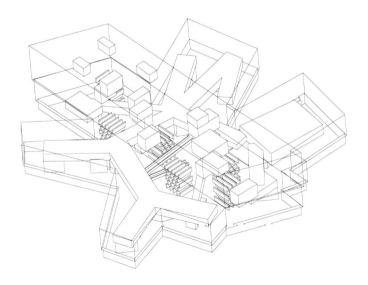

Organizational diagrams

TOP: Information space

BOTTOM: Inhabitable space

Site perspective

TOP: Model view (interior)

BOTTOM: Model detail (exterior)

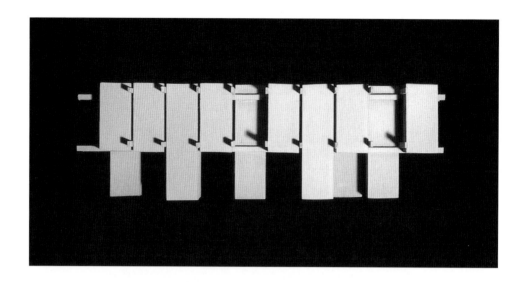

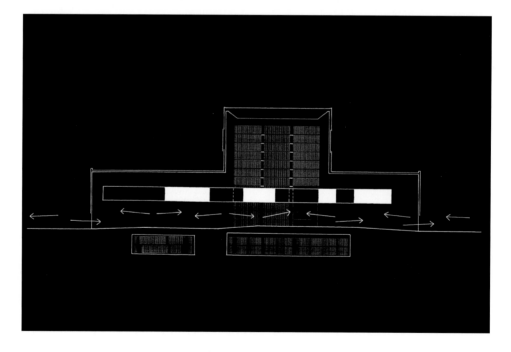

TOP: Stack model

BOTTOM: Section diagram

TOP: Section

BOTTOM: Detail of exterior cladding

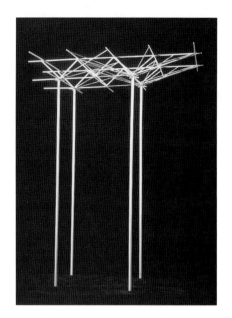

132

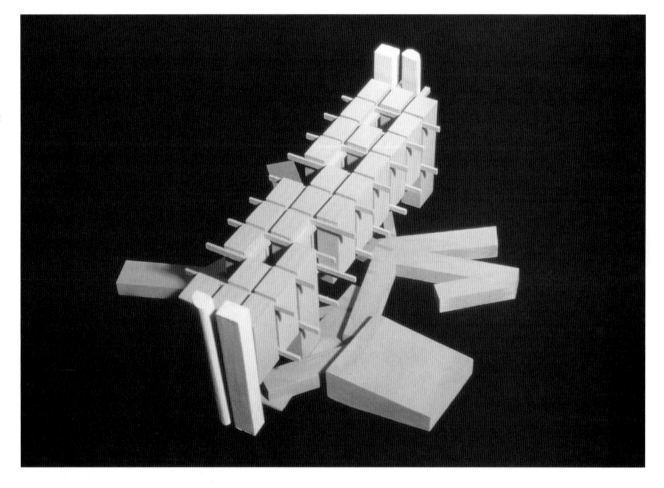

TOP: **Structural model**

BOTTOM: **Stack layout**

OPPOSITE: **Stack model**

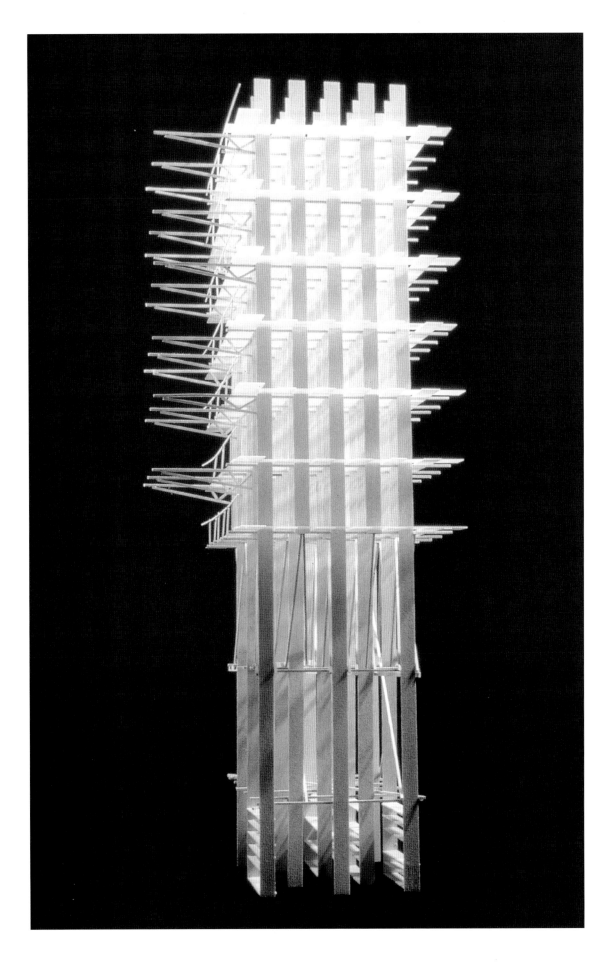

Field Conditions KANSAI

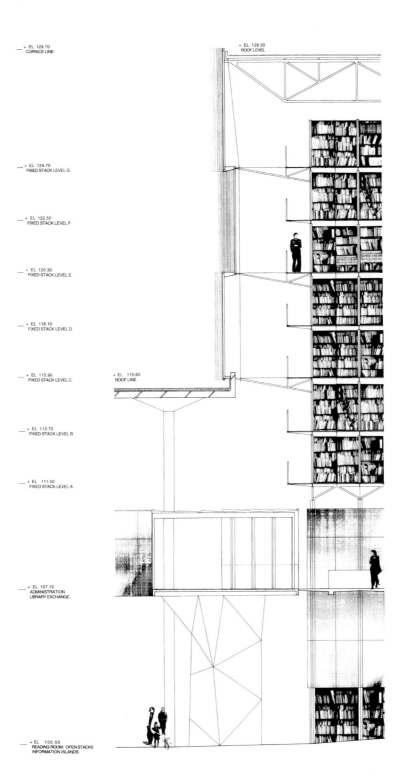

+ EL 129.70
CORNICE LINE

+ EL 129.20
ROOF LEVEL

+ EL 124.70
FIXED STACK LEVEL G

+ EL 122.50
FIXED STACK LEVEL F

+ EL 120.30
FIXED STACK LEVEL E

+ EL 118.10
FIXED STACK LEVEL D

+ EL 115.90
FIXED STACK LEVEL C

+ EL 115.60
ROOF LINE

134

+ EL 113.70
FIXED STACK LEVEL B

+ EL 111.50
FIXED STACK LEVEL A

+ EL 107.10
ADMINISTRATION
LIBRARY EXCHANGE

+ EL 100.50
READING ROOM: OPEN STACKS
INFORMATION ISLANDS

ABOVE: Section detail

OPPOSITE: Model view: section

Urbanism without Architecture

R. E. SOMOL

The organs distribute themselves on the BwO [Body without Organs], but they distribute themselves independently of the form of the organism; forms become contingent, organs are no longer anything more than intensities that are produced, flows, thresholds, and gradients....It is a problem not of ideology, but of pure matter. —GILLES DELEUZE AND FELIX GUATTARI

Artificial landscape without cultural precedent began to dawn on me. —TONY SMITH

If it would not exaggerate his centrality or condemn him to obsolescence, one might imprudently suggest that Stan Allen—collector and connoisseur, cataloger and codifier—is at once our Philip Johnson and our Colin Rowe. Now, before the objections begin, one would quickly have to offer the caveats: rather than producing the visible signature of pastiche, there is here the systematic anonymity of the seamless; in place of the timeless articulation of figure-ground formalism, the intensive field of an operative *informalism*. In the end it is difficult to *see* Allen's work, to get a read on what it looks like. Some will say that the six competition projects collected here are "not much," while for others they will be "a little bit of everything"; for some there may be "no architecture," for others work that is "extremely diagrammatic." But it is doubtful anyone will recognize the significance of what they have said. Perhaps Allen's fate is to become our Zelig, to assimilate with various surroundings, a legendary case of architectural psychasthenia: "he is similar, not similar to something, but just *similar*."[1]

As an active critic and promoter of both his predecessors and contemporaries, it is quite possible that no one has a broader understanding of international design practices today than Stan Allen. It is this familiarity with the field—almost his dispersed identity through the field—that enables him to navigate the various impasses that characterize contemporary disciplinary debate, moving shrewdly between the oppositional polemics of the European minimalists of the box and the American organicists of the blob, the moralists of traditional craft and the avatars of digital media, the celebrants of building tectonics and the defenders of social and environmental responsibility. In this way, Allen's projects successfully solicit and consolidate a series of heretofore incompatible traits: default regularity and supple continuity, refined physical models as well as abstract notations and visualizations, repetitive structural elements alongside organizations borrowed from landscape ecology.

Just as Daniel Libeskind's "Three Lessons in Architecture" codified the critical insights offered by the first generation neo-avant-garde, Allen's machines and propositions have institutionalized the projective techniques of the second generation, most notably from the work of Libeskind himself, Bernard Tschumi, and Rem Koolhaas. In this way, the thrust of his work appears to follow the shift from semiotic critique to institutional projection, and explains why — given that the polemics of current architecture are played out

Sequence of Gausian blurs

between the terms *plastic* and *infrastructural*, or *formal* and *operational*, or *representational* and *performative*—his work appears to align itself with the practices that privilege the latter over the former. The situation, however, is not so simple, as anyone who takes notice of the great amount of discourse that accompanies the work should already suspect. As an alternative to *tectonics*, which attempts to subsume a projected opposition between rhetoric and construction, a genuinely *diagrammatic* practice needs to be understood as a hybrid of the early neo-avant-garde investigation of signifying regimes with the later pursuit of new institutional arrangements. As opposed to the tectonic vision of architecture as the legible sign of construction—which is intended to resist any potential status as either commodity or cultural speculation—a diagrammatic practice (flowing around obstacles yet resisting nothing) multiplies signifying processes (technological as well as linguistic) within a plenum of matter, recognizing signs as complicit in the construction of specific social machines.

The role of the architect in this model is dissipated, as he or she becomes an organizer and channeler of information, since rather than being limited to the decidedly vertical—the control and resistance of gravity, a calculation of statics and load—"forces" emerge as horizontal and nonspecific (economic, political, cultural, local, and global). And it is by means of the diagram that these new matters and activities—along with their diverse ecologies and multiplicities—can be made visible and related. One of the crucial contributions of Allen's various "material concepts" is that architecture can engage larger and more complex scales, but only through abstract modes of representation and notation. The "real" practice of architecture is already constituted by vast documents of abstraction—building and tax codes, market projections and interest rates, ordinances and zoning laws, actuarial tables and demographic statistics—and these are all aspects of the materials of construction. Thus, an engagement with "the real" does not imply some return to an imaginary essence (i.e., the "ontology of

138

construction") or to the experientially subjective atomism of flaccid phenomenologies. A diagrammatic practice exposes the conditions and activates the opportunities implicit in recognizing that the real is already a site of the virtual.

Allen reconstructs the neo-avant-garde as a linked consortium of machines rather than as a series of exceptional individuals, as operations more than monuments, as cogs in the machine of a possible future practice. In coming to repeat and institutionalize the project of his predecessors, he frames this work in terms of what Michel Foucault would refer to as "statements." Statements, in effect, are the discursive aspect of institutions (which are the nondiscursive corollary to statements), and have a peculiar connection to repetition.

> Instead of something being said once and for all…the statement, as it emerges in its materiality, appears with a status, enters various fields of use, is subjected to transferences or modifications, is integrated into operations and strategies in which its identity is maintained or effaced. Thus the statement circulates, is used, disappears, allows or prevents the realization of a desire, serves or resists various interests, participates in challenge or struggle, and becomes a theme of appropriation or rivalry.[2]

In Allen's work, language and sign systems emerge as social and political machines. As described in Gilles Deleuze's analysis of Foucault, statements occupy a different space than either propositions (which are typological and vertical) or phrases (dialectical and horizontal); they are topological and diagonal. And although statements may be rare,

> no originality is needed to produce them. A statement always represents a transmission of particular elements distributed in a corresponding space. As we shall see, the formations and transformations of these spaces themselves pose topological problems that cannot adequately be described in terms of creation, beginning or foundation. When studying a particular space, it matters even less whether a statement has taken place for the first time, or whether it involves repetition or reproduction. What counts is the regularity of the statement: it represents not the average but rather the whole statistical curve.[3]

From this observation, one can begin to account for the speed-sampling in Allen's projects, where citation is dissolved as informational excess, erasing both edges and gaps as well as any trace of signature. Like the dumb enumeration of the alphabetical order adopted by the typewriter—*QWERTY*—Allen's projects are "statements" of this kind, a machinic interface of tool and language, work that does not copy in the traditional sense, but rather plots "the whole statistical curve."[4] It is perhaps in this way that Allen perceives the affinity of his own work to that of MVRDV, reading it as he does through the machinic writing technique of Raymond Roussel.[5] And it is finally this statistical orientation that leads both MVRDV and Allen to the metropolis as the site for a collective architecture, with the city now viewed through the lens of infrastructure.

Allen's infrastructural vision (or his solicitation of the urban unconscious) begins as early as his work on the Campo Marzio, and continues through the scores for the London Project, the instrumentalization of Dziga Vertov's montage, and the collaborative design research in the Croton Aqueduct study. In fact, the historical trajectory that this work charts—from Piranesi to film to minimalism—consistently reveals a secret history of dark space, a program associated with architectural and urban poché, with infrastructure. Against the cubist-gestalt opticality of rigid figure-ground dialectics—or the positive public space visualized by the Nolli plan—Allen proposes the intensification of field-field combinations, the potential emergence of the figure in the endlessness of the moiré or through the entropy of the gradient. And this unconscious or emergent figuration is less a phenomenon of an increasing "bigness" (typologically associated, for example, with the skyscraper) than of a progressive *slackening* (evident in the more horizontal types of malls, airports, casinos, etc.). Thus, his architecture of the "loose fit" mimics posturban sprawl, a relaxation of boundaries that informs a practice that will be referred to here as *urbanism without architecture* (UwA). For the condition of posturbanism is marked not by the disappearance of the metropolitan, but by the proliferation of the urban *everywhere*. Today, as "urban design" has disappeared as a distinct but limited discourse, a range of new fields have emerged which go by the names *landscape urbanism, interior urbanism*, and even *infrastructure urbanism*, a triad of terms that leave far behind the suffixes "design" and "architecture" that had once regulated disciplinary identification and legitimacy. Finally, this UwA operates as an alternative both to the historical options of the City Beautiful and the CIAM, as well as to the more recent advocates of a New Urbanism or to their discontents among the social critics and geographers of the contemporary city.

The interwar project of modernist urbanism attempted to discipline the city with architecture, to bring metropolitan chaos under control via building, plans, and codes. Today, with the dispersal of the city, with the reorganization of the urban at other levels (both global and cybernetic), architecture has returned, conversely, as sublimated chaos absorbed by a market that had previously been characterized by confusion but which has now been rendered, via corporate-statist intervention, as simply consumerist. Against the "speculative" (of both commercial development and formal experimentation), and in an uncanny reprise of the CIAM, the New Urbanists, too, attempt to "fix" urbanism with architecture, an attempt that leads with equal if opposite force to the predilection for a particular style. Literalizing the metaphor of urban planners before them, they seek to *architecturalize* the city, to see the city as a big (classical or modernist) building, a device of discipline and order. In contrast, work like that of Allen and others condenses the effects of the city and captures or channels its energies, and in this way architecture *becomes* infrastructure rather than serving as

140

either monumental figure or infill fabric. This infrastructural attitude is often figured through a liberated roof element—variously characterized as "large," "open," "vast," and "continuous"—a structure at once extensive and intensive, as in the projects for the Prado (the early competition version), Beirut, and Barcelona. Without endorsing the *strategy* of master planning or its parallel abandonment through the minor interventions suggested by *tactics*, Allen's projects engage the excessive and eccentric opportunities afforded by *logistics*: urbanism without the regrets.

It is precisely this logistical deployment of materials—this celebration of exchange—that distinguishes Allen's speculations from the urban resentment that infiltrates the ideology critique of contemporary social geographers and theorists. Whereas Edward Soja develops a profound distrust of the exopolis, "the city without,"[6] Allen ventures to extend the urban organizational logics manifest in cities like Los Angeles, as evidenced in his Korean-American Museum of Art entry which operates as a kind of condenser of sprawl where public space emerges as residual, casually disposed between service systems and a now interiorized landscape. KOMA, in other words, explores the opportunities and possibilities offered by the "continuous urban field" where "homes, offices, factories, and shopping malls float in a culturing medium,"[7] conditions that have been perhaps too readily dismissed by critics like Michael Sorkin. Whereas an earlier project like the Cardiff Bay entry maintains a commitment to the compositional logic of a collage or montage aesthetic, the box-in-box organization of KOMA activates

interstitial mat spaces. Contrary to the early work of, say, Frank Gehry or John Hejduk, the program figures are here given a consistency to float within, thus figuring the negatively characterized "culturing medium" of Sorkin's sprawl. Similarly, Allen's work explicitly accelerates the effects of what Trevor Boddy critiques as the "analogous city," an urbanism of infrastructure (e.g., tunnels and bridges) that Boddy perceives as a dangerous deviation from the authentic public life of the traditional city.[8] While Boddy can only nostalgically recall public life grounded on the planimetric determinacy of radial or gridded streets—i.e., infrastructure as the frame of a legible urban gestalt—Allen pursues the publicity of the urban section, a thickened surface often characterized by a composite infrastructure (as with the structural layer cake of KOMA, which combines parallel concrete walls and a differentiated truss system).

In a continuous if more defined way than the social critics and geographers represented in Sorkin's collection *Variations on a Theme Park*, Albert Pope has recently described contemporary posturban or exurban organizations as "not random 'sprawl,' but a radical, discontinuous or distributed unity."[9] For Pope, in other words, there is a method (diabolical though it may be) to this seeming madness:

> It has been shown that residential subdivisions, office parks, commercial malls, airports, skywalks, high-rise sections and freeways all apparently issue from the same template. This apparent unity

of form is extraordinary given the present conception of contemporary urban development as so much uncontrolled and disorganized "sprawl." That the majority of urban elements share a common order across a broad range of scales suggests a totality which remains completely obscure to popular perceptions of the city. The implications of such "transparent" forms of organization are, to say the least, socially and politically suspect....To promote the entropic disorganization of the city and the complete collapse of metropolitan representation could amount to nothing more than an enormous evasion of responsibility.[10]

Despite Pope's plea, Allen's work suggests that it is precisely architecture's forty-year obsession with representation (whether in the guise of postmodernism or deconstructivism), as well as its reciprocally destitute call for a return to a simplified "reality," that constitutes architecture's true irresponsibility. Rather than rely on the vertical interface of architecture as the device for a recognizable public life—one that articulates differences between interior and exterior, public and private, figure and ground, and so on—Allen's UwA wagers on a more performative role where architecture acts as a medium for the continuous horizontal exchange between natural and artificial ecologies, internal and external activities. While an extensive roof organization has been one technique for this operation in his larger urban proposals, his institutional projects enact this exchange through the trope of provisional envelops or excessive wrappers. Rather than identifying architecture with "the wall," Allen, along with others in the field, realigns the discipline toward the metropolitan flows associated more readily with infrastructure, the landscape, and the interior.

This reorientation of contemporary architectural ambitions can also be seen in two of the entries to the 1997–98 competition for a student center on Mies van der Rohe's IIT campus. While OMA proposes a completely contingent envelop that produces an intensive interior urbanism, Peter Eisenman's scheme buries the student center beneath a modulated prairie landscape. In both instances—whether the project becomes all interior or all landscape—the traditional, representational or institutional identification of architecture with the wall is displaced. Without bifurcating these options, Allen's earlier entry for the Kansai National Diet Library produces an emergent "information garden," where the reading room and landscape are continuous organizations mediated by the provisional figure of the envelope, itself a hybrid natural/artificial skin filtering daylight and electronic information. This tactic of the fuzzy edge is perhaps most fully developed in the generic, barcode urbanism of the Prado entry where the addition emerges as a continuation of the gardens, one which mixes indiscriminately with the endless inversion of institutional striations that make up the primary blocks of entry and auditorium, galleries, and library.

Against an optical, gestalt model of architecture and urbanism where figure-field relations are heightened and articulated to the point where they become domesticated as figure-ground balance, Stan Allen's recent work has been systematically experimenting

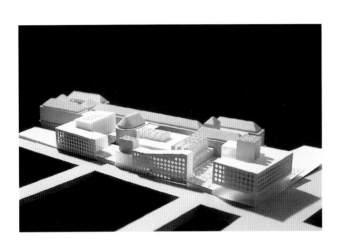

Museo del Prado, Madrid, (project), 1995–98. Model

Allen's work only matters after dark, in that historical moment when the metropolis is no longer constrained by its visible, hierarchical parts, but is stimulated by the stochastic motion of disparate multiplicities dancing across its surfaces, provoking speculative arrangements at once commercial *and* critical. Like Visa and the id, UwA is everywhere you want to be.

with an alternative orientation of potentially endless and entropic field-field organizations. This proliferation of backgrounds not only allows a reassessment of those fields of operation once considered peripheral to architecture proper (i.e., landscape, interiors, and infrastructure), but equally provides for a new way to imagine and arrange collective, urban activities. Allen's projects represent the disciplined response to the immanent urbanism of the film *Pulp Fiction*, where all the significant events unfold in bathrooms and cars, in the blind spots of architectural and urban poché. As with Tony Smith's late night drive on the unfinished and abandoned infrastructure of the New Jersey Turnpike, or Donald Judd's version of the statistical curve—"simply order, one thing after another"—Stan

NOTES

1. Roger Caillois, "Mimicry and Legendary Psychasthenia," *October* 31 (winter 1984): 30.
2. Michel Foucault, *The Archaeology of Knowledge and the Discourse on Language* (New York: Pantheon Books, 1972), 105.
3. Gilles Deleuze, *Foucault* (Minneapolis: University of Minnesota Press, 1988), 3–4.
4. Foucault, *The Archaeology of Knowledge*, n. 3, 86.
5. Stan Allen, "Artificial Ecologies: The Work of MVRDV," *El Croquis* 86 (1997): 26–33.
6. See Soja, "Inside Exopolis: Scenes from Orange County," in *Variations on a Theme Park*, ed. Michael Sorkin (New York: Noonday Press, 1992).
7. Sorkin, introduction to *Variations on a Theme Park*, xii.
8. See Trevor Boddy, "Underground and Overhead: Building the Analogous City," also published in *Sorkin's Variations on a Theme Park*, 152: "We should sound alarms at all radical urban interventions that portray themselves as 'just' infrastructure."
9. Albert Pope, *Ladders* (New York: Princeton Architectural Press, 1996), 222.
10. Ibid., 222, 224.

Stan Allen: Chronology

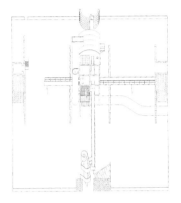

Axonometric

**Shinkenchiku Residential Design,
(competition: honorable mention), 1981**
PUBLISHED: *Japan Architect* (February 1982): 42–3.

Site plan

New Orleans Museum of Art Competition, project, 1983
WITH: Marc Hacker

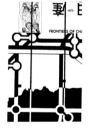

Detail of city score

The London Project, 1986
WITH: Marc Hacker
EXHIBITED: The London Projects, Artists Space, New York, 1986.
PUBLISHED: *The London Projects* (New York: Princeton Architec-
                       tural Press, 1988), section 6.
                       Janet Abrams, "New York Looks at London," *Blue-
                       print* (March 1987): 46–7.

Projection

**"Piranesi Campo Marzio" (1986–89), Architecture for the Year
2001 (competition), Tokyo, 1985. Second prize.**
PUBLISHED: *Japan Architect* and *A+U,* joint edition, (summer,
                       1985): 44–5.
                       Victoria Geibel, "Harbingers of Change," *Metropolis*
                       (May 1987): 46–56.
                       "In the Labyrinth: After Piranesi and Robbe-Grillet,"
                       The Pratt Journal of Architecture V, II (1989): 55–8.
                       "Piranesi's *Campo Marzio:* An Experimental Design,"
                       Assemblage 10 (1989): 71–109.
                       Contemporary Architectural Drawings (New York:
                       Avery Library Centennial, 1992), 7.

Amy Lipton Gallery, New York, 1989–91

EXHIBITED: *Between Drawing and Building*, Ross Gallery,
Columbia University, 1991.

PUBLISHED: "40 under 40," *Interiors* (September 1995), 53.
Between Drawing and Building (New York: Columbia University, 1991).
Patricia Phillips, untitled review, *Artforum International* (October, 1991): 10, 131.
"Drawing/Model/Text," *Architecture and Urbanism* (April 1992): 40–67.

Exhibition space

fiction/nonfiction Gallery, New York, 1990

EXHIBITED: *Between Drawing and Building*, Ross Gallery,
Columbia University, 1991.

PUBLISHED: *Between Drawing and Building* (New York: Columbia University, 1991).
Patricia Phillips, untitled review, *Artforum International* (October, 1991): 10, 131.
"Drawing/Model/Text," *Architecture and Urbanism* (April 1992): 40–67.

Exhibition space

White Columns Gallery, New York, 1990–91

EXHIBITED: *Between Drawing and Building*, Ross Gallery,
Columbia University, 1991.

PUBLISHED: *Between Drawing and Building* (New York: Columbia University, 1991).
Patricia Phillips, untitled review, *Artforum International* (October, 1991): 10, 131.
"Drawing/Model/Text," *Architecture and Urbanism* (April 1992): 40–67.

Elevation

Able House, Abingdon, PA, 1991–92

PUBLISHED: "On Projection," *Harvard Architectural Review* 9 (1993): 122–37.
"Drawing/Model/Text," *Architecture and Urbanism* (April 1992): 40–67.

Pivot door: detail

Arning loft (renovation), New York, 1991

PUBLISHED: Beverly Russell, ed., *Forty under Forty* (Grand Rapids, MI: Vitae Press, 1995), 96–8.
Casa Brutus (spring–summer 1996): 32–3.

Section detail

Venice Competition, 1991

WITH: Jesse Reiser and Nanako Umemoto

PUBLISHED: "It's Exercise, under Certain Conditions," *D: Columbia Documents* 3 (1993): 89–113.

Architecture of Shadows, project for the Choragic Monument Competition, New York City Chapter, American Institute of Architects, 1990. Honorable mention; revised 1992.

PUBLISHED: "An Architecture of Shadows," *Semiotext(e) Architecture* (1992), np.

Perspective

Demarcating Lines, Beirut, 1992

PUBLISHED: "Hotel in Beirut," *Arquitectura* (Mexico City), (1992) 42–5.

"It's Exercise, Under Certain Conditions," *D: Columbia Documents* 3 (1993): 89–113.

"Young Architects in New York," *Space Design* (September 1992): 68–71.

Croton Aqueduct Study, 1992–95

WITH: RAAUm Group: (Jesse Reiser, Polly Apfelbaum, Stan Allen, Nanako Umemoto)

EXHIBITED: *City Speculations*, Queens Museum of Art, New York, 1995.

PUBLISHED: "It's Exercise, under Certain Conditions," *D: Columbia Documents* 3 (1993): 89–113.

"A New East Coast Movement," *Space Design* (March 1994): 41–3.

Patricia C. Phillips, ed., *City Speculations* (New York: Princeton Architectural Press, 1996), 72–7.

"Folding in Architecture," *Architectural Design* 102 (1993): 86–9.

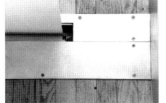

Screen detail

Miller/Minter Loft, New York, 1993–96

ASSISTED BY: Katherine Kim

PUBLISHED: Julie V. Iovine, "Repose," *New York Times Home Design Magazine*, April 1996, 32–3.

Detail

Fertig Loft, renovation, 1993

ASSISTED BY: Katherine Kim

PUBLISHED: Darleen Bungey, "Globetrotter's Loft," *House and Garden* (November 1996): 142–7.

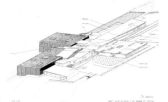
Axonometric view

Estonia Museum of Art, Tallinn, Estonia, (competition), 1994
PUBLISHED: "A New Generation of Architects," *Space Journal*
             329 (March 1995): 62–71.
             "Designing on the Computer," *Arch* + 128 (September 1995): 38–9.

Cardiff Bay Opera House, Cardiff, Wales, (competition), 1994
ASSISTED BY: Jack Phillips and Katherine Kim
PUBLISHED: "Take Four," *World Architecture* 42 (January 1996):
              106–9.
              Ben van Berkel and Caroline Bos, "The Young Americans," *AA Files* 29 (June 1995): 79–83.

Reconstruction of the Souks of Beirut, (competition), 1994
ASSISTED BY: Jack Phillips and Katherine Kim
PUBLISHED: Lynnette Widder, "The Margins of Error," *Diadalos*
              59 (March 1996) 122–7.
              "The Power of Architecture" *Architectural Design*
              114 (1995): 88–91.
              "A New Generation of Architects," *Space Journal*
              329 (March 1995) 62–71.

148

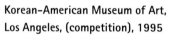
Interior view

Avery Computer Studios, New York, 1994
ASSISTED BY: Lyn Rice, Katherine Kim, Anna Mueller
PUBLISHED: "A New Generation of Architects," *Space Journal*
              329 (March 1995) 62–71.
              Beverly Russell, ed., *Forty Under Forty* (Vitae Press,
              1995), 96–8.
              "Designing on the Computer," *Arch* + 128 (September 1995): 38–9.

Korean–American Museum of Art,
Los Angeles, (competition), 1995
ASSISTED BY: Lyn Rice, Katherine Kim, Chris Perry
MODEL BY: Michael Silver
PUBLISHED: "Korean-American Museum of Art," *Architectural
              Design* 128 (1997): 66–9.
              "Games of Architecture," *Architectural Design* 121
              (1996): 21.

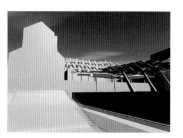

Perspective, 1995

Museo del Prado, Madrid, Spain, (competition), 1995/98
ASSISTED BY: Andrew Burges, Martin Felsen, Galia Salomonoff;
              computer renderings by David Ruy. Reworked 1998;
              assisted by Chris Perry, Marcel Baumgartner
PUBLISHED: "Museo del Prado," *AP Architectural Projects* (June
              1996): 40–7.

Entry/reception

Zabriskie Gallery, New York, 1995
ASSISTED BY: Lyn Rice, Katherine Kim

Gordon/Wolfe Loft, New York, (renovation), 1996
ASSISTED BY: Lyn Rice, Martin Felsen

Barcelona ZAL, Barcelona, Spain, (competition), 1996
ASSISTED BY: Céline Parmentier, Adriana Nacheva, Troels
                        Rugbjerg, Nona Yehia
PUBLISHED: *Concursos/Competitions UIA Barcelona 1996* (cata-
                        log of finalists), (Barcelona: UIA, 1997), 28.
                        "Infrastructural Urbanism," *Scroope* 9 (1996): 71–9.
                        "Performance Notations: Barcelona ZAL," in *Open
                        City,* ed. John Knechtel (Toronto: Alphabet City, 1998).

National Diet Library, Kansai Kan, Japan, (competition), 1996
ASSISTED BY: Tsuto Sakamoto, Mieko Sakamoto, Troels Rugbjerg
PUBLISHED: *A+U* (August 1998).

149

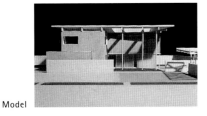
Model

LB House, Los Angeles, 1997
ASSISTED BY: David Erdman, Katherine Kim, Tsuto Sakamoto,
                        Nona Yehia, Chris Perry

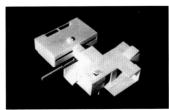

Model

**Diao House, Addition to a 1949 Marcel Breuer House,
New York State, 1998 –**
ASSISTED BY: Chris Perry

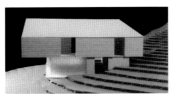

Model

Miller / Minter House, Cold Spring, NY, 1998–
ASSISTED BY: Marcel Baumgartner

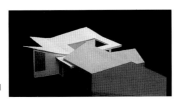
Model

**VZ House Addition,
East Hampton, NY, 1998–**
ASSISTED BY: Chris Perry

Acknowledgments

Architecture is a collaborative art form, and many people contributed to the work published here.

In particular, I would like to thank Kenneth Frampton and Rafael Moneo for their advice and support; K. Michael Hays and R. E. Somol for their uncanny abilities to turn apparent liabilities into assets; the students and colleagues at the Columbia University Graduate School of Architecture, Preservation and Planning who have continually pushed me to clarify and refine the ideas presented here, and Bernard Tschumi who is responsible for that fertile mix; all those who have worked in my office, among them: Marcel Baumgartner, Martin Felsen, Katherine Kim, Anna Mueller, Adriana Nacheva, Céline Parmentier, Chris Perry, Jack Phillips, Lyn Rice, Troels Rugbjerg, Mieko Sakamoto, Tsuto Sakamoto, Michael Silver, and Nona Yehia; Katrin Kalden and Mariano Desmarás for preliminary design work; Marta Falkowska for image research; Kevin Lippert, Mark Lamster, and Sara Stemen of Princeton Architectural Press for their careful work on this book; and most of all, Polly Apfelbaum for patience and an infallible eye.

Illustration Credits